*Prosperity isn't about wishing for wealth.
It's about learning the language of money.*

THE
POWER
TO
PROSPERITY

TJ HILL

Published by TJ HILL
Paperback ISBN: 979-8-994139400
eBook ISBN: 979-8-994139417
Special Edition
Printed in the United States of America
For information, permissions, or inquiries, contact:
www.tjhillbooks.com

Book Cover by SK Lynne

Cataloging-in-Publication Data
Hill, T.J.
The Power to Prosperity: A Powerful Guide to Gain Unlimited Prosperity Through Planning and Focus / by TJ Hill.
Subjects: Success in business | Personal finance | Goal setting | Self-development

Contents

TJ Hill

Prosperity isn't about wishing for wealth. It's about learning the language of money—and teaching yourself to think in it. When you understand that language, prosperity stops being luck, and starts being literacy.

Introduction

One of the most basic human ambitions is a desire for wealth. Every person aspires to live a full and abundant life, and contemporary civilization has made the quest of affluence its defining characteristic. However, being rich isn't always simple. Finding one's way is difficult for many individuals, and the path to riches is often paved with difficulties and difficulties.

The good news is that everyone may enjoy wealth. It is not only for the fortunate few, but rather for those who are prepared to put in a lot of effort, make wise plans, and concentrate their efforts. This effective manual is made to assist people in achieving limitless success through preparation and dedication. It is a step-by-step guide to success in all facets of life, from relationships and job to money and personal development.

Part 1: The Power of Planning

Success is built on a foundation of planning. It is difficult to do anything of importance without a plan. The power of planning will be examined in this part of the manual in order to show how it may assist people in achieving unrestricted prosperity.

Establishing your definition of prosperity is the first step in creating a strategy towards it. What are your aims and goals? What goals do you have for your work, income, interpersonal connections, and personal development?

You may start developing a strategy for accomplishing your goals after you have a clear understanding of what you desire.

The last stage is to divide your objectives into doable tasks. This entails determining the precise steps you must take to accomplish your objectives. For instance, if your objective is to launch a profitable firm, your activities may involve gathering market data, creating a business strategy, and obtaining capital.

Prioritizing your tasks is crucial once you have identified them. This entails deciding which chores should be completed right now and which ones can wait. Setting priorities may help you maintain focus and make sure you are moving in the direction of your objectives.

Part 2: The Focusing Power

Another essential component of success is focus. Without concentration, it is simple to become sidetracked and forget your objectives. The power of concentration will be discussed in this chapter of the manual, along with how it might enable people to experience limitless affluence.

The first step in learning to concentrate is to get rid of distractions. This is figuring out how to get rid of the items in your life that are diverting your focus from your objectives. You can think about restricting your usage of social media, for instance, if you discover that you are using it excessively.

Making a routine that supports your objectives is the next stage. This entails creating routines and behaviors that support your objectives and keep you on track. A regimen that incorporates regular exercise and a balanced diet may be created if, for instance, your objective is to enhance your physical health.

Part 3: Removing Barriers

There will always be challenges on your path to success, no matter how well you prepare and maintain your focus. In this portion of the book, we'll look at some typical challenges and solutions.

Fear is one of the most prevalent barriers. Fear may be a strong force that prevents us from reaching our objectives. The secret to getting over fear is to confront it head-on. This entails facing your concerns head-on and taking action to do so. For instance, if you're nervous of speaking in front of groups, you may sign up for a public speaking class or join a Toastmasters club to practice.

The absence of funding is another frequent barrier. This may include time, money, or access to vital relationships and networks. It's crucial to have creative solutions on hand to get beyond this difficulty. This entails solving your challenges creatively and making the most of your available resources. For instance, if you need to generate money for your company, you may want to think about crowdsourcing or looking for investors that share your goals.

Finally, it's critical to understand that obstacles and failures are a normal part of the path to success. Nobody succeeds without facing obstacles and failing along the way. The important thing is to take what you can from them and apply it to further your development.

Part 4: The Value of Continuous Learning

The quest for wealth requires ongoing learning and development. The ability to adapt and change along with the environment around them is a prerequisite for success. The need of ongoing education and methods for remaining current with trends are also covered in this part of the manual.

Being educated is one of the best ways to remain on top of things. This entails staying current with news and developments in your sector or business. It also entails keeping up with emerging trends and technology that might affect your line of work.

Finding mentors and role models is another crucial tactic. Learning from others who have succeeded before you may be a very effective technique to get knowledge and direction. Look for mentors that have excelled in fields that are important to you and who share your ideals.

Chapter 1
Defining Prosperity

What is Prosperity?

The word "prosperity" is frequently used to refer to a condition of happiness, success, and affluence. It includes a wide range of dimensions of life, such as material prosperity, individual development, and society advancement. Even though it might be challenging to define and quantify prosperity, it is typically thought of as a desirable state of being that many people aim to attain.

Prosperity is fundamentally linked to a growing economy and financial affluence. This is due to the fact that access to resources and financial security are frequently regarded as essential elements of a good existence. This might entail having a steady employment, a good salary, and the capacity to take care of one's fundamental necessities without experiencing too much worry or strain. People typically feel more empowered to pursue their objectives, take chances, and engage in their own personal growth and development when they are financially secure.

Prosperity, though, involves more than simply material wealth. Additionally, it is about developing and fulfilling oneself. People with a feeling of purpose and direction in their life are frequently ones who feel fortunate. They experience a strong sense of community, are linked to others, and find meaning and purpose in their job and other endeavors. This might involve things like engaging in interests or hobbies, giving back to the community, or supporting a cause or purpose that is important to them.

In the end, prosperity is a multidimensional idea that covers a wide range of facets of life. Although it is a crucial element, financial stability is not the sole one. Those who are able to find meaning and purpose in their life and who make an effort to improve the world for everyone are frequently those who are genuinely successful.

Being able to assess and quantify success might be one of the main obstacles to reaching it. While monetary riches and economic expansion are rather straightforward to gauge, other facets of success, such as societal advancement and personal contentment, are more challenging to evaluate. It can be challenging to pinpoint places where development is required and to create successful plans for fostering prosperity as a consequence.

Despite these difficulties, there are several methods for people and communities to strive to advance prosperity. Investing in education and skill development, encouraging entrepreneurship and innovation, and trying to build a more inclusive and fair society are a few examples of what this might include. Additionally, it might entail promoting sustainable development that protects the environment for future generations as well as trying to eradicate poverty and injustice.

In the end, prosperity is a target worth pursuing on both a personal and communal level. Even though it may be challenging to do, it is doable with the correct attitude, tools, and assistance. We can build a society where everyone has the possibility to have a meaningful life and where everyone has the ability to contribute to the greater good by working together to promote prosperity.

Defining YOUR Personal Definition of Prosperity

The idea of prosperity has been around for many years, and it is often related to riches, success, and plenty. However, prosperity is a relative concept that depends on the individual. Having a clear grasp of what you want to accomplish in life and how you want to live it allows you to define your own unique definition of prosperity, which is essential.

Finding the aspects of life that are most important to you in your life can help you define your unique concept of success. Financial success, a fruitful job, a happy family life, excellent health, or any combination of these might qualify. Once you've determined what success means to you, you can begin taking steps to make it a reality.

One of the biggest advantages of setting your own definition of success is that it gives you focus and direction. You may create objectives and go toward them with purpose and clarity when you are certain of what you want to accomplish. You can focus your time and resources and make better choices as a result of this clarity.

For instance, if achieving financial success is your idea of wealth, you may choose to concentrate your efforts on advancing your job or launching a company. You may make investments, establish financial goals, and develop a budget to help you reach your goals. On the other hand, if your idea of prosperity revolves on your family, you could place a higher value on spending time with them and cultivating close bonds with them.

Having a clear understanding of what success means to you personally may also help you remain motivated and get over challenges. When you are focused and driven, even in the midst of difficulties, you are more likely to have a clear objective in mind. This drive enables you to persevere through challenges and strive toward reaching your goals.

Furthermore, coming up with your own idea of prosperity might make your life more rewarding. Knowing what is important to you allows you to live a life that is meaningful to you and to behave in a way that is consistent with your beliefs. A happier and more meaningful life may result from this alignment, which offers you a feeling of fulfillment and purpose.

It's crucial to understand that coming up with your own concept of prosperity is a continuous process. Your idea of prosperity may alter as you mature and develop. It's critical to frequently review your definition of prosperity and make any required modifications.

In conclusion, figuring out your own concept of prosperity is essential to success and a happy existence. It offers concentration, drive, direction, and a feeling of purpose. Spend some time figuring out what success means to you, then work with purpose and intention to get there. Remember that leading a prosperous life is about more than simply having money and material belongings; it's about having a meaningful and full existence.

Setting Clear Financial Goals to Achieve Prosperity

To various individuals, financial success might mean different things. It could entail living comfortably without worrying about money for some people, while it might involve obtaining a specific degree of wealth or financial independence for others. Whatever your idea of financial wealth may be, one thing is for certain: obtaining it requires having certain financial objectives.

You may better identify what you want to do, why you want to accomplish it, and how you intend to accomplish it by setting clear financial objectives. It gives your financial journey direction, meaning, and drive you in maintaining your commitment to your objectives.

Here are some pointers on how to establish precise financial objectives in order to prosper:

<u>Set financial objectives:</u> Start by stating what you understand financial success to imply. Do you wish to invest in a company, pay off your debts, or save for a down payment on a home? Whatever your objectives may be, put them in writing and be as detailed as possible about what you want to accomplish, how much money you need, and when.

<u>Prioritize your objectives.</u> After you've determined your financial objectives, rank them in order of significance and urgency. Some objectives would need to be accomplished right now, like paying off high-interest debt, while others can be long-term, like investing for retirement. You may direct your efforts and resources to the most important goals first by prioritizing your objectives.

<u>Plan:</u> After you've prioritized your objectives, come up with a strategy for achieving them. This strategy should include the precise actions you must take, such as raising your income, cutting down on your spending, or making the correct financial investments. Be realistic about the amounts of time and money needed to complete each task, and make changes as necessary along the way.

Follow your development: By reviewing your plan often and keeping track of your earnings, outgoing costs, savings, and investments, you can monitor your progress toward your financial objectives. This will keep you motivated as you see yourself moving closer to your objectives and help you discover any gaps or places where improvements need to be made.

Maintain your discipline: Financial success involves tenacity, patience, and discipline. It's crucial to remain dedicated to your objectives and to resist temptations or diversions that might thwart your progress. In order to do this, you may have to make some short-term sacrifices, including reducing wasteful spending or putting in more overtime to earn more money.

Consult a financial expert if you need assistance creating a plan or have questions about how to reach your financial objectives. You may examine your financial state, spot possibilities and hazards, and create a tailored strategy that fits your objectives and values with the aid of a financial adviser or planner.

Gaining success depends on having certain financial objectives. You may get closer to your financial objectives and reach the wealth you want by clearly defining your objectives, setting priorities, developing a strategy, tracking your results, maintaining discipline, and getting expert help. Keep in mind that achieving financial wealth is a journey that calls for constant work and dedication. You can reach your financial objectives and lead the life you desire if you have the appropriate perspective and strategy.

The Role of Visualization and Positive Thinking in Achieving Prosperity

Positive thinking and visualization are effective strategies for achieving success. Being prosperous may be characterized as a condition of prosperity, thriving, and plenty in several facets of life, including the material, psychological, and spiritual. The use of visualization and positive thinking may assist people in overcoming challenges, altering limiting beliefs and developing a more upbeat attitude on life, all of which can eventually result in financial success.

Creating mental pictures of what one wishes to accomplish is called visualization. Visualization may assist people in concentrating on their objectives and forming a distinct image of what they want to accomplish. The subconscious mind is activated when someone visualizes their objectives; this subconscious mind then starts to work towards obtaining those goals. Numerous aspects of life, such as work, relationships, and personal growth, may benefit from visualization.

For instance, someone who wishes to become financially prosperous might utilize visualization by seeing oneself as having a large sum of money in their bank account, a luxury house, and a fancy automobile. The person might start to think that this is achievable and start taking steps to realize their objectives by forming this mental picture and repeatedly envisioning them. The effectiveness of visualization comes in its ability to help people concentrate on their objectives, which may inspire them to take action in that direction.

Yet another effective method for achieving riches is positive thinking. Positivity and a focus on good events, feelings, and ideas are also components of positive thinking. Positive thinking may aid people in overcoming limiting ideas, anxieties, and uncertainties that may stand in the way of their success.

For instance, someone who desires to establish a company could have unfavorable notions about their ability or deserving of success. By concentrating on affirmations that are uplifting, such as "I am capable of achieving my goals" or "I am worthy of success," positive thinking may assist individuals in overcoming negative beliefs. The person may develop a more optimistic attitude on their skills and take steps to realize their objectives by concentrating on positive thoughts and emotions.

Together, visualization and optimistic thinking may help people develop a strong attitude that will help them flourish. A person develops a strong belief system that supports their aims when they imagine their objectives and put them together with positive thinking. This way of thinking keeps people motivated to accomplish their objectives while assisting them in overcoming challenges and disappointments.

Additionally, people may attract riches into their life by using visualization and positive thought. According to the law of attraction, people may attract everything they put their attention on into their life. People may attract the resources, chances, and people they need to accomplish their objectives by thinking positively and envisioning them.

In conclusion, it is impossible to stress the importance of vision and optimistic thinking for reaching success. People may use visualization and positive thinking as effective techniques to get rid of limiting beliefs, have a good view on life, and attract wealth into their lives. Individuals may succeed in many aspects of life and have successful, full lives by combining these skills with action.

Developing a Comprehensive Financial Plan for Achieving Prosperity

Laying financial objectives, developing a budget, controlling debt, laying aside money for emergencies and retirement, and making investments for the future are all part of a complete financial plan, which serves as a road map for success. For people and families that wish to attain long-term financial independence and security, it is a crucial tool.

Setting financial objectives is the first step in creating a thorough financial strategy. This entails deciding on both short- and long-term goals, including purchasing a house, paying off debt, setting aside money for retirement or launching a company. Goals must be precise, quantifiable, doable, relevant, and time bound. Individuals may concentrate their efforts and develop a strategy that is specific to their requirements by defining clear objectives.

After deciding on financial objectives, the following step is to make a budget. A budget outlines how money will be distributed among costs. To understand where money is being spent and find areas where expenditure may be cut, it is crucial to keep track of costs. A realistic budget should account for all sources of income and outgoing costs, including both fixed costs like utilities, insurance, and rent or mortgage payments as well as variable costs like food, entertainment, and travel.

A thorough financial plan must include debt management as a key component. Debt may be a burden that restricts one's financial independence and keeps people from reaching their objectives. Creating a strategy to pay off debt, such as credit card bills, a school loan, or a mortgage, is crucial. This might include debt consolidation or negotiating lower interest rates or monthly payments with creditors.

Another key component of a thorough financial strategy is emergency savings. A financial safety net may help people weather unforeseen calamities like job loss, sickness, or natural disasters. Emergencies can arise at any moment. A decent general rule of thumb is to have three to six months' worth of expenditures saved up.

A key component of long-term financial security is retirement planning. A retirement savings strategy, such as making contributions to an IRA or 401(k), should be part of a comprehensive financial plan. To maximize the impact of compound interest, it's crucial to begin retirement savings early.

Another crucial element of a thorough financial strategy is investing for the future. In order to get a return on investment, investors place funds into stocks, bonds, or other assets. Over time, investing may assist people in accumulating money, but it's crucial to recognize the dangers and, if necessary, seek expert guidance.

It is crucial to have expert guidance from a financial counselor or planner when creating a thorough financial strategy. A specialist may assist people with setting financial objectives, developing budgets, controlling debt, saving for emergencies and retirement, and making investments for the future. They may also provide advice on other financial issues, such as tax planning and estate preparation.

Success can only be attained by creating a thorough financial strategy. It includes making a budget, defining financial objectives, controlling debt, putting money away for unexpected expenses and retirement, and making investments in the future. Individuals may design a strategy that meets their requirements and aids in their long-term financial independence by using these stages and expert counsel.

The Power of Habits and Routines in Achieving Prosperity

Routines and habits are effective strategies that may significantly aid in obtaining success. They serve as the foundation for our everyday existence, guiding our conduct and affecting our ideas and deeds. People that are successful recognize the value of creating routines and habits that support their objectives. They understand that success and realizing one's potential need discipline, commitment, and consistency.

Ability to boost productivity and efficiency is one of the main advantages of forming healthy habits and routines. We give our life structure and a feeling of order when we adopt routines. This may enable us to prioritize our tasks and more effectively manage our time and resources. For instance, we are more likely to be productive throughout the day and accomplish our objectives if we create a pattern of rising early, working exercise, and preparing our day.

The fact that routines and habits might help people feel less stressed and anxious is a significant advantage. We don't need to spend mental energy making decisions after we have established patterns of conduct. We minimize our cognitive burden and free up brain space for more critical duties since we know what to do and when to do it. Routines may also provide one a sense of stability and comfort, which can lessen emotions of uncertainty and worry.

Routines and habits may significantly contribute to the development of a successful attitude and set of behaviors when it comes to obtaining wealth. For instance, successful individuals often follow routines related to their own growth, such as daily meditation or reading. They could also practice behaviors related to their jobs, such as prioritizing their duties and making objectives. They may acquire the knowledge and mentality required to flourish by constantly participating in these practices.

Creating healthy routines and habits may be challenging since it can be challenging to maintain them over time. It's simple to relapse into old routines or become sidetracked by other concerns. There are methods, nevertheless, that may help us improve our odds of success. Starting small and gaining momentum gradually is a successful tactic. We may start with a simple habit and add to it gradually rather than attempting to build a complicated routine all at once. This may assist us in acquiring the steadiness and self-control required to uphold our habits over time.

Making our routines and habits a priority in our life is another smart move. This entails reserving time and money to carry out the actions that advance our objectives. If we want to establish a pattern centered on fitness, for instance, we can block out time in our calendar to go to the gym or go running. Making our routines and habits a priority will increase the likelihood that we will follow them and get the desired outcomes.

The strength of routines and habits ultimately rests in their capacity to mold our actions and affect the results. We may boost our productivity, lessen stress and anxiety, and build the abilities and attitude required to flourish by forming good habits and routines that are in line with our objectives and desires. Long-term regular maintenance requires commitment and discipline, but the rewards are well worth the effort.

Chapter 2
Self-Discipline

The Importance of Self-Discipline in Achieving Prosperity

A key component of both personal and professional development and the achievement of success is self-discipline. Even in the face of challenges or diversions, it is a trait that enables people to maintain their concentration on their goals and objectives. In other terms, self-discipline is the capacity to exert self-control and adhere to a plan or routine devoid of outside influences.

Since it enables people to form the positive habits required for success, self- discipline is crucial for wealth. Self-control, for instance, helps people to work hard and endure despite obstacles or disappointments. It supports individuals in maintaining a positive outlook and a strong work ethic, both of which are essential for success.

Additionally, self-control enables people to make wiser choices and refrain from impulsive actions that might obstruct their advancement. It enables people to concentrate on the long-term effects of their activities as opposed to instant gratification or rewards. Self-control enables people to make moral decisions that are consistent with their objectives and beliefs.

Self-control also aids people in efficiently managing their time and resources, which is another factor in wealth. Disciplined people are more likely to prioritize their activities, establish realistic objectives, and use their time effectively. Additionally, they are more likely to make prudent use of their resources and refrain from squandering time or money on pursuits that do not advance their general prosperity.

Self-control also aids in fostering a feeling of accountability and duty in people. Disciplined people take responsibility for their actions and are more inclined to accept blame for their triumphs and mistakes. Additionally, they tend to be more dependable and trustworthy, which may aid in developing lasting connections and expanding their possibilities for success.

Self-control also aids people in overcoming procrastination and moving toward their objectives more swiftly. Disciplined people are less inclined to procrastinate or put off doing something. They are more inclined to act and get closer to their objectives, which might hasten their path to riches.

Finally, adopting a development mentality requires self-discipline. Disciplined people are more inclined to rise to difficulties and gain knowledge from their mistakes. Additionally, they are more inclined to look for novel possibilities and take chances that can result in higher success. Self-discipline aids people in creating a growth-oriented attitude that may result in long-term success.

In conclusion, developing self-control is essential for prospering. It aids people in creating positive habits, improving their decision-making, time and resource management, accepting accountability for their actions, overcoming procrastination, and cultivating a growth mindset. Therefore, those who wish to flourish should learn self-control and make it a regular part of their lives. They may accomplish their objectives and build a life of prosperity and joy by doing this.

The Role of Perseverance and Determination in Achieving Prosperity

To flourish, one must have two qualities: perseverance and determination. Focus, discipline, and tenacity in the face of difficulty are essential for success in any activity. Success is seldom attained by performing a single, simple activity or action; rather, it is attained via a succession of gradual advances over time. The secret to sustaining momentum and advancement toward one's objectives is perseverance and tenacity.

The act of pursuing a goal or target despite difficulties or failures is known as perseverance. It calls for a degree of mental toughness and tenacity that might be difficult to sustain over time. The most successful people, however, are often those who endure despite adversity. This is due to the fact that they are able to stay motivated and focused even under trying circumstances.

Another significant quality that is necessary for obtaining riches is determination. It entails a readiness to exert the effort and labor required, despite potential obstacles, to attain one's objectives. People who are determined to succeed are prepared to make concessions, put in extra effort, and overcome challenges. Setbacks or failures don't readily dissuade them; instead, they utilize them as chances to develop and learn.

Perseverance and tenacity make up a potent duo that may aid people in achieving success in all spheres of life. These two traits are essential for success in all endeavors, whether they be in business, sports, academia, or interpersonal relationships. When things become difficult, those who possess them are able to maintain their concentration and motivation.

The life of J.K. Rowling, the author of the Harry Potter series, serves as one illustration of the strength of tenacity. Rowling overcame a lot of obstacles in her life before breaking into the best-selling book category. She was a single mother living on assistance, battled depression, and had a tense relationship with her ex-husband. Rowling stayed committed to her objective of becoming a writer despite these challenges. She wrote manuscripts for publishers for years, sending them, and being rejected time and time again. But she persisted, and her perseverance ultimately paid off. She is now among the best-selling writers of all time, with more than 500 million copies of her works having been sold globally.

The life of Michael Jordan serves as another illustration of the strength of tenacity. Although Michael Jordan is considered as one of the best basketball players of all time, his success was not uncomplicated. Jordan was a young basketball player who was dismissed from his high school squad. He utilized the setback as inspiration to work harder and advance his abilities rather than give up on his goal of becoming a professional player. Later on, he was given a scholarship to play basketball in college, and he went on to have a famous NBA career during which he won six championships and a staggering number of individual honors.

Perseverance and tenacity were crucial in each of these cases for obtaining riches. Both Jordan and Rowling are unlikely to have achieved their goals of being famous basketball players or renowned authors without these characteristics. Even in the face of failures and difficulties, these people were able to stay motivated and focused, and they eventually succeeded in achieving their objectives through tenacity and perseverance.

Finally, it should be noted that persistence and tenacity are crucial traits for reaching success in all spheres of life. These two qualities are essential for success in all endeavors, whether they be in business, sports, academia, or interpersonal relationships. People that have them are able to stay motivated and focused despite challenges in order to work hard and persevere until their objectives are attained. Therefore, it is crucial for people to develop these traits inside themselves and to utilize them as a base for realizing their goals and leading productive lives.

The Power of Networking and Building Relationships for Achieving Prosperity

It is impossible to overestimate the importance of networking and establishing contacts for obtaining riches. Success in every industry relies not just on one's knowledge and abilities but also on the professional networks one develops. Whether you are a corporate leader, an entrepreneur, or a professional in any industry, networking and developing contacts may help you advance your career and find more success.

Building connections and relationships with individuals in your business, community, or area of interest is the goal of networking. Anyone who wants to widen their network, discover fresh possibilities, and build lasting connections might benefit from using it. Through networking, you may make new friends, discover market trends, and acquire knowledge about your sector.

Establishing connections is crucial to networking. Relationships are the cornerstone of every successful collaboration because they are based on mutual respect, trust, and understanding. The ability to create credibility and win others' confidence via the development of good connections may open up new doors for possibilities and partnerships.

You may become prosperous in a number of ways by networking and developing connections. The first benefit is that it might aid in your job search. You may discover fresh job vacancies, learn about the hiring process, and even be referred for positions that might not be publicly publicized by growing your network and cultivating connections with individuals in your sector.

Second, networking may aid in company expansion. You may broaden your market and accelerate the growth of your company by establishing connections with new customers, partners, and investors. You may learn about new technology, obtain market knowledge, and keep up with industry trends via networking.

Third, networking might enable you to get mentoring and advice from seasoned experts. By forming connections with individuals who have more experience than you, you may benefit from their knowledge, obtain insightful knowledge, and get advice that will help you reach your objectives more quickly.

Fourth, networking may boost your exposure and make you more noticeable in your field. You may network with new people, display your talents and knowledge, and even deliver presentations that can position you as an authority in your profession by going to industry events, conferences, and seminars.

And last, networking and developing contacts may support the development of a powerful personal brand. You may draw in new customers, partners, and even job opportunities by making a good first impression and establishing yourself as a reputable expert in your sector.

You need excellent communication skills, the capacity for active listening, and the willingness to assist others if you want to be successful at networking and developing connections. Networking is about more than simply meeting new people; it's also about creating enduring connections based on respect, trust, and understanding.

In conclusion, there is no way to emphasize the importance of networking and establishing connections for earning riches. Whether you are an executive in business, an entrepreneur, or a professional in any industry, networking and developing contacts may help you succeed more, discover new possibilities, and forge lasting alliances that can advance your firm or career. Spend money on networking and developing relationships, and then watch as your career or company soars.

The Importance of Continuous Learning and Self-Improvement For Achieving Prosperity

Achieving success in one's personal and professional life depends on ongoing learning and self-improvement. The world is evolving continually, and individuals who can't keep up with these changes risk being left behind. People may put themselves in a position to take advantage of new possibilities, stay competitive in the job market, and improve their general quality of life by committing to lifelong learning and self-improvement.

Keeping up with the most recent developments and trends in one's profession is one of the main advantages of continuous learning. For instance, employees who are unable to keep up with the most recent digital tools and platforms run the danger of slipping behind their colleagues in today's quickly expanding technical scene. On the other hand, people who are always learning and looking to broaden their skill set will be better able to adapt to shifting circumstances and seize new chances as they present themselves.

The ability to increase one's productivity and effectiveness in everyday life is another important advantage of continual learning. People may increase their productivity at work and be more accurate and timely with their job by continually learning new methods and strategies. As a result, people may have more time for leisure activities and might attain a better work-life balance.

Continuous learning may have a substantial influence on personal development in addition to its professional advantages. People may expand their horizons and get a better understanding of the world around them, for instance, by taking up new activities, languages, or cultures.

Similar to this, people may improve their general quality of life and create more satisfying interactions with others by pursuing personal development objectives like developing their communication skills or practicing mindfulness.

It's important to remember, however, that self-improvement and ongoing learning may sometimes be difficult. Finding the time and motivation to pursue new objectives may be challenging, particularly if one is already overcommitted with family and job commitments. Additionally, learning and developing may be difficult processes since they often require people to venture outside of their comfort zones and face unfamiliar concepts or viewpoints.

Despite these difficulties, the advantages of lifelong learning and self- improvement make the effort worthwhile. Online courses, books, and local seminars or workshops are just a few of the tools available to aid people in achieving their objectives. To assist their staff members keep current with market developments, many businesses also provide training and development opportunities.

It is impossible to overestimate the significance of lifelong learning and development for reaching success. People may position themselves for success in both their personal and professional lives by making a commitment to lifelong learning and working to better themselves. Even if the process may not always be simple, the benefits of development and self-improvement make the effort worthwhile.

How to Overcome Fear and Uncertainty When Pursuing Prosperity

We may often be prevented from seeking success by fear and uncertainty. Reaching our greatest potential might be hampered by fears such as failure, the unknown and taking chances. However, there are methods to get past these worries and doubts so that you may confidently seek wealth.

Determine your Apprehensions and Doubts

Finding out what is generating your anxiety and doubt is the first step to conquering them. It may be the fear of making a mistake, the fear of being rejected, or the worry of running out of money. You may start creating a strategy to get over your fear after you've determined what it's really made of.

When attempting to achieve riches, setting reasonable objectives is crucial. You are more prone to feel dread and uncertainty when you have unattainable ambitions since they appear so far away. Instead, make tiny, attainable objectives that you can achieve over time to give you momentum and confidence.

Make a Strategy

It's time to make a strategy when you've recognized your worries and uncertainties and established reasonable objectives. Along with a schedule for when you intend to accomplish your objectives, your plan should include the measures you must take to do so. Your objectives may seem more reasonable and doable if you divide them into smaller, achievable stages.

Do Something

The most crucial step in overcoming fear and uncertainty is taking action. No matter how much you plan and prepare, nothing will change until you act. Start with the simple actions specified in your strategy, and then gradually advance to greater and more difficult objectives. Just keep in mind that any development is still progress.

Accept Failure

Failure comes naturally on the path to success. Consider failure a chance to learn and develop rather than something to be afraid of. Every setback provides an opportunity to identify what doesn't work and change your strategy appropriately. Keep in mind that failure is only a bump in the road on the route to success; it does not define you or your ability.

Seek Assistance

It doesn't have to be a lonely trip to pursue riches, but it may be. Ask for help from close friends, family, or a mentor who can provide direction and inspiration along the road. You may remain motivated and goal-focused by surrounding yourself with positive and encouraging individuals.

Engage in Self-Care

It is crucial to look for one while aiming for riches. Make sure you are getting enough sleep, eating a healthy diet, and doing things that make you happy and relax. When you are in good physical and mental health, you are more capable of overcoming the obstacles that come with achieving riches.

Conclusion: When chasing wealth, anxiety and uncertainty are normal feelings, but they don't have to stop you. You may get over these feelings and pursue wealth with confidence by acknowledging your anxieties, establishing reasonable objectives, making a strategy, acting, accepting failure, getting help, and taking care of yourself. The road to success is not a straight one; rather, it is a series of ups and downs. You may succeed and have a successful life if you are persistent and determined.

Chapter 3
Beliefs & Mindset

The Importance of Taking Calculated Risks to Achieve Prosperity

Taking calculated risks is necessary to flourish in life. Life requires taking chances, and without them, we would never advance or be successful. Though not all risks are equal, taking careless chances might result in failure and letdown. Take sensible risks in order to increase your chances of success and financial prosperity.

Taking a gamble after assessing the advantages and disadvantages of the circumstance is known as calculated risk. Making wise selections needs thorough consideration of the prospective consequences. It entails assessing the issue, compiling pertinent information, and taking into account every eventuality that could occur. It entails weighing the likelihood of success against the chance of failure and deciding whether the possible reward justifies the risk.

People may flourish in a variety of aspects of their lives, such as their employment, income, relationships, and personal development, by taking measured risks. Entrepreneurs that are successful in business often take calculated risks to do so. To expand their enterprises, they research industry trends, spot possible possibilities, and take measured risks. For instance, after studying the market and customer demand, a company owner may decide to invest in a new product line. If the investment is successful, it may result in more wealth and earnings.

Similar to this, taking prudent risks may result in career progress and growth. For instance, a worker could take on a difficult project or change roles to acquire new knowledge and experiences. These measured risks may result in job success, pay raises, and promotions.

Taking calculated chances with one's money might also result in success. For instance, after thorough consideration and study, a person can decide to invest in the stock market or launch a company. If the investment is successful, it could result in prosperity and financial security. It's important to remember, however, that taking measured risks entails managing risk as well. Investment diversification, having a safety net, and avoiding dangers that may put one in financial disaster are crucial.

Taking measured risks in relationships may result in personal development and stronger connections. For instance, people could risk being open and vulnerable in order to improve their relationships. This might include opening up about delicate subjects, expressing one's feelings, or taking the chance of forgiving someone who has wronged them. These measured risks may result in deeper connections, more intimate relationships, and a more satisfying existence.

Prosperity may result from taking reasonable risks for personal development. People could, for instance, take the chance of venturing outside of their comfort zones in order to explore new things or follow their hobbies. This might include picking up a new activity, going on a solo trip, or establishing a new business. These measured risks may result in personal development, boosted self-esteem, and a more contented existence.

Taking prudent risks is crucial to living a prosperous life, to sum up. It requires thorough research, assessing the pros and cons, and deliberative decision-making. It may result in achievement and prosperity in a variety of spheres of life, including work, relationships, wealth, and personal development. But it's essential to control risk, stay away from careless hazards, and have a safety net in place. People may advance in life, flourish, and prosper by taking measured risks.

How To Identify and Eliminate Limiting Beliefs that Hinder Prosperity

Beliefs that restrict our potential to succeed and obstruct our success are those that we have about ourselves, other people, or the world at large. We may not even be aware of their existence or how they affect our lives since they can become so deeply embedded in our subconscious brains. But if we want to succeed and flourish in our life, we must recognize and get rid of limiting ideas. Here are some actions you may take to find and get rid of limiting ideas that prevent financial success.

Learn to recognize your beliefs.

Being aware of limiting ideas is the first step towards recognizing and eradicating them. Spend some time thinking about your attitudes, actions, and cognitive processes. What do you think about wealth, achievement, and prosperity? Do you think it's difficult to find money? Do you think that some people are just fortunate enough to succeed? Do you think success is something you don't deserve?

Question your beliefs.

The next stage is to confront your limiting beliefs when you've discovered them. Are you sure this view is true? Are there any proofs that back it up? Limiting beliefs sometimes stem from presumptions or previous experiences that may not be accurate or applicable to your present circumstance. For instance, if you think it's difficult to get money, question that notion by considering if it's really true. Examine any persons in your life who appear to be naturally drawn to wealth? What steps can you take to make your life more prosperous?

Change constricting beliefs with liberating ones.

It's time to confront your limiting beliefs and then swap them out for powerful ones. Beliefs that are empowering help you succeed and flourish by supporting your aims. For instance, you may adopt the idea that money comes to you quickly and in plenty in lieu of the thought that money is difficult to get by. If you work hard and remain focused, you may replace the notion that success is solely for the fortunate few with the idea that success is something you can achieve.

Make a move.

Although it's a crucial first step, recognizing and eliminating limiting ideas is insufficient by itself. To make your new beliefs a reality, you must act. Set objectives that are consistent with your new beliefs and take action to accomplish them to start. Start taking steps to attract more money into your life, such as beginning a side company or investing in stocks, if you now feel that money comes to you readily and abundantly.

Try to surround oneself with uplifting people.

You may reinforce your new views and maintain your motivation to accomplish your objectives by surrounding yourself with good influencers. Avoid those that pull you down or reinforce your limiting views and look for those who are encouraging of your aims and ideals. Additionally, you may read books, listen to podcasts, or go to seminars that encourage growth-oriented thinking.

In other words, if you want to succeed and be wealthy in your life, you must recognize and get rid of limiting ideas that prevent prosperity. You may overcome the restrictions that have been holding you back and design the life you actually want by being conscious of your beliefs, confronting them, swapping them out with empowering ones, acting, and surrounding yourself with good influences. Keep in mind that your beliefs determine the world you experience.

The Role of Creativity and Innovation in Achieving Prosperity

Innovation and creativity are two critical elements that are essential to creating prosperity for people, businesses, and societies as a whole. Innovation is the process of turning these ideas into useful applications that benefit society, while creativity is the capacity to generate novel ideas, solutions, and approaches to issues. When creativity and invention are fostered and promoted, they may result in improved living conditions, burgeoning economies, and higher levels of productivity. The importance of innovation and creativity in creating wealth is covered here.

First of all, innovation and creativity result in the development of fresh goods and services that benefit society. Companies must develop unique goods in a highly competitive market to keep one step ahead of their rivals. Innovation not only results in the development of new items but also enhances the functionality and value of already existing goods and services. Companies may open up new markets, boost sales, and boost profits when they can innovate and develop new goods. As more people have access to new and improved goods and services, the economy becomes richer as a consequence.

Second, innovation and creativity are critical to raising production. People and organizations are more likely to come up with new and improved methods of doing things when they are encouraged to be creative and inventive. This results in more effectiveness, lower costs, and better performance. For instance, using new technology and manufacturing procedures may result in quicker production cycles, better-quality goods, and reduced prices. Similar to this, using innovative teaching techniques in the classroom may help students get better results and increase their chances of succeeding in the workplace. As consumers have access to better products and services at reduced costs, increased productivity promotes economic development and raises living standards.

Thirdly, innovation and creativity may result in the emergence of new markets and employment possibilities. New industries are born and old ones grow when new goods and services are developed. This generates employment chances for individuals with various backgrounds and skill sets, resulting in a more varied and dynamic workforce. The development of new industries also draws both local and international investment, resulting in economic growth and greater wealth for the entire country.

Fourthly, innovation and creativity may help to make social and environmental situations better. A cleaner and more sustainable environment may be achieved, for instance, by reducing greenhouse gas emissions with the use of new technology in renewable energy. The same is true for new medical technology, which may raise the standard of treatment and thereby enhance people's and communities' health. The development of new social policies and initiatives, including those for affordable housing and educational opportunities, may also result from innovation.

In conclusion, success in today's world of fast change depends on creativity and innovation. New industries and employment possibilities are produced as a result of them, and social and environmental circumstances are also improved. They also raise productivity. Governments, businesses, and people should support innovation and creativity in all spheres of life, from business and policymaking to research and education. By doing this, we can ensure both our own prosperity and the sustainability of future generations.

Developing a Success Mindset for Achieving Prosperity

One of the most important aspects of obtaining riches in life is having a success attitude. A person with a success mentality is able to have an optimistic attitude on life, establish realistic objectives, and persistently strive toward those goals. We will go through how to cultivate a success attitude for material wealth in this book.

Have faith in yourself. Belief in oneself is the first step in acquiring a success attitude. You have to have confidence that you can succeed and that you have the knowledge and skills required. The basis of a successful attitude is self-belief. You are more willing to take chances, attempt new things, and persevere through difficulties when you have confidence in yourself.

Establish precise objectives. You must have certain objectives if you want to be prosperous. Setting goals gives you focus and direction. Without objectives, life would be a pointless journey. Make sure your objectives are SMART (specific, measurable, attainable, relevant, and time-bound) when you establish them. You'll be able to maintain motivation and concentrate if you have SMART objectives.

Create an optimistic outlook. Gaining a success mentality requires having a good attitude. You may remain motivated, have an optimistic view, and find the good in any circumstance if you have a positive attitude. Good individuals and opportunities are more likely to come into your life when you have a good outlook.

Accept Failure is a natural part of life and a necessary step on the road to achievement. You must accept failure and see it as a teaching opportunity if you want to cultivate a success attitude. After failing, instead of giving up, look at it as an opportunity to improve. Examine your errors, learn from them, and try again after making improvements.

Become growth-oriented. A growth mindset is the conviction that you can learn and develop through perseverance and hard effort. Being prosperous requires having this perspective since it enables you to perceive setbacks as chances for personal development. You are more likely to accept challenges, persevere through hurdles, and accomplish your objectives when you have a growth mentality.

Be in the company of uplifting individuals. Your thinking and your life are greatly influenced by the people you spend time with. Spend time with positive individuals who support your objectives and dreams if you want to create a success attitude. You will be inspired and motivated to be your best self by positive individuals.

Do something finally; you need to act if you want to build a success attitude. Setting objectives and maintaining a good mindset are insufficient. You must consistently take action to achieve your objectives. The secret to success is action. Your aspirations and objectives will only become reality if you take action.

Conclusion: Achieving affluence requires having a success attitude. A success mentality helps you to have confidence in yourself, establish specific goals, have an optimistic outlook, accept failure, cultivate a growth mindset, surround yourself with inspiring others, and take action to achieve your objectives. You may cultivate a success attitude and succeed in every aspect of your life by adhering to these principles.

The Power of Gratitude and Appreciation in Achieving Prosperity

Two strong feelings, gratitude and appreciation, may have a significant influence on many aspects of our life, including our capacity for success. Prosperity is about enjoying plenty in all facets of life, including health, relationships, and personal development. It is not simply about amassing money or material stuff. By cultivating thankfulness and appreciation, we turn our attention from what we lack to what we already have and create space for even more abundance to enter our lives.

Being grateful supports us in developing a good mentality, which is one of the many reasons it is so effective. By concentrating on our blessings, we teach our minds to see the silver lining in any circumstance. This optimistic mindset may assist us in attracting more favorable possibilities and experiences into our life. We become more open to the richness that is waiting for us when we recognize the riches that already exists in our life.

On the road to riches, gratitude may also assist us in overcoming hardships and stumbling blocks. It's simple to get frustrated after failures or setbacks and lose focus on our objectives. But when we express thankfulness, we are reminded of all the benefits in our life and are given the fortitude and resiliency to go on. When we are grateful, we are more likely to see failures as chances for development and learning than as obstacles to our achievement.

Gratitude may assist us in developing a good outlook as well as enhancing our interpersonal connections. By showing others our thankfulness and appreciation, we strengthen our bonds and foster a climate of mutual respect and trust. More chances for cooperation, assistance, and mutual success may result from this. By appreciating others' efforts, we start a beneficial circle of reciprocity where everyone benefits from the success of the group.

Another effective method for creating success is appreciation. We are better able to use the opportunities and resources we have to double our plenty when we recognize their worth. For instance, if we value knowledge, we are more likely to put up the time and energy necessary to acquire new skills or pursue further education. We are more inclined to take care of our bodies via exercise and diet if we recognize the significance of our health. We become better stewards of the opportunities and resources in our life by appreciating them, which may eventually result in more success.

Additionally, gratitude might enable us to live lives that are more meaningful and fulfilled. We are more inclined to seek out and create more of the people and events that make us happy when we show appreciation for them. We make decisions that are in line with our beliefs and aspirations as we become more aware of our passions and interests. Living an appreciative life gives us a feeling of contentment and purpose that transcends worldly affluence.

It is impossible to overestimate the importance of appreciation and thankfulness for earning wealth. These two feelings support us in developing a positive outlook, overcoming obstacles, enhancing our relationships, and leading more rewarding lives. The door to more wealth in all spheres of life is opened when we concentrate on what we have rather than what we lack. Everyday acts of thankfulness and appreciation help us build a tremendous momentum of good energy that drives us forward toward our objectives and aspirations.

Chapter 4
Financial Literacy

The Importance of Financial Literacy in Achieving Prosperity

A crucial component of both individual and society success is financial literacy. It alludes to the capacity to comprehend and successfully handle one's financial concerns. It entails obtaining the information and abilities required to handle financial choices including budgeting, saving, investing, and debt management.

For people, families, companies, and even whole economies to prosper, financial literacy is essential.

One of the main advantages of financial literacy is that it gives people the authority to manage their money. People who are financially literate are better able to comprehend and manage their money, make wise financial choices, and steer clear of expensive errors. They may, for instance, build a budget, establish financial objectives, and decide on borrowing and investing wisely. Better financial results follow, including higher savings rates, lower debt levels, and higher credit ratings.

For individuals who are vulnerable or at a disadvantage economically, financial literacy is especially crucial. These populations are particularly vulnerable to financial exploitation, con artists, and predatory lending practices because they may lack access to financial resources or have inadequate financial literacy. They may better safeguard themselves and their family from financial damage and enhance their economic well-being by increasing their financial literacy.

Additionally essential to fostering stability and economic progress is financial literacy. Financial literacy makes people and companies better able to participate in the economy and make wise financial choices. They are more likely to raise their spending and investment in their enterprises, save more money for retirement, and support the national economy. In turn, this fosters stability, economic development, and job creation.

Financial literacy is also necessary for creating a society that is more equal. Financial inequality is a widespread issue that may have serious social and economic repercussions in many nations. People from all walks of life may gain the information and abilities necessary to manage their money wisely and accumulate wealth over time by increasing their financial literacy. This may therefore lead to a smaller wealth gap and more economic equality.

For retirement and long-term financial planning, financial literacy is also essential. Many individuals have trouble making financial plans, which may result in financial instability and even destitution in old life. People may better prepare for retirement, invest in the future, and manage their money by increasing their financial literacy. By easing the strain on social safety nets and fostering more economic stability, this may guarantee a secure and successful retirement.

A vital component of both individual and community success is financial knowledge. It encourages economic development and stability, empowers people to manage their money, and works toward a more just society. We can promote higher financial well-being and create a more successful and resilient economy by enhancing financial literacy via education and awareness-raising initiatives.

Developing a Diverse Income Stream to Achieve Prosperity

Achieving affluence requires diversifying your sources of income, particularly in the dynamic economic environment of today. A person who depends only on one source of income, such as a full-time work or a single company endeavor, may be more susceptible to market fluctuations, problems unique to a particular sector, and unforeseen failures. On the other side, creating various sources of income may provide a feeling of stability and security in your finances as well as the chance to make more money.

One of the key advantages of having many sources of income is that it promotes more adaptability and flexibility. Having other streams of income, for instance, might lessen the financial burden in the event that one source of income decreases or disappears totally. Additionally, diversifying one's sources of income enables one to follow a variety of hobbies and passions, which can be both personally enjoyable and financially rewarding.

Diverse revenue streams may be created in a variety of ways. To explore various jobs or freelancing possibilities is one strategy. This might include working various part-time jobs or taking on contract work in addition to a full-time employment. As an alternative, people might look into chances to work independently or as consultants in their fields of expertise, serving a range of clientele.

Investing in assets that provide passive income is another approach to create a variety of income streams. This may apply to stock, bond, and other types of investments, as well as real estate investments. For instance, owning rental property may provide a consistent flow of rental income, while buying dividend-paying stocks can result in recurring dividend payments.

Additionally a potential alternative for creating many sources of income is entrepreneurship. Starting a company or many firms may provide the chance to follow one's hobbies and passions while also offering the possibility for large revenue. The development of e-commerce and online marketplaces has made launching a company easier and more inexpensive than before.

The sustainability and scalability of each source of revenue should be taken into account while creating varied income streams. It's critical to evaluate each possibility and take into account variables including market demand, rivalry, and possible profitability. To avoid overstretching oneself or passing up one opportunity in favor of another, it's crucial to strike a balance between the time and resources needed for each source of revenue.

Prioritizing passive income sources over active ones is another thing to think about since they demand less time and effort. While active income sources, like consulting or freelancing, might bring in money right away, passive income sources can eventually bring in money that is more steady and predictable.

Finally, while creating many revenue sources, it's critical to be adaptive and flexible. The economic environment is continuously changing, so an option that is lucrative now may not be viable tomorrow. It's critical to keep up with market trends, economic indicators, and new possibilities, and to be prepared to change course and modify one's income sources as necessary.

In conclusion, obtaining affluence in the current economic climate requires diversifying one's revenue sources. People may expand their earning potential, lessen their financial susceptibility, and follow their hobbies and interests by pursuing numerous sources of income. Creating numerous revenue sources requires careful study, evaluation, and adaptation, whether by working several jobs, passive income investments, or self-employment. Individuals may attain more financial security and success in the years to come by taking a proactive approach to income generating.

The Importance of Saving and Investing for Achieving Prosperity

Two essential elements of reaching financial wealth are saving and investing. While saving helps people accumulate a cash reserve to cover their immediate and short- term requirements, investing is essential for long-term wealth growth. To ensure future financial security and stability, investing and saving go hand in hand.

It is impossible to emphasize the value of saving. To achieve financial stability and keep debt at bay, you must have a savings strategy. A healthy savings account may provide as a safety net in case of unanticipated circumstances like job loss, urgent medical needs, and unplanned bills. People may make sure they have enough money to pay their debts off, cover their payments, and buy goods they desire or need by saving money.

Additionally, saving might assist people in achieving their long-term financial objectives. Saving money over time is crucial to accomplishing these objectives, whether you're saving for a down payment on a home, a child's education, or retirement. Compound interest, which indicates that the interest received on savings will also yield interest, may be used by those who consistently save money. This may accelerate the growth of their savings and help them get closer to their financial objectives.

On the other hand, investing is crucial for long-term wealth growth. The act of investing is the practice of placing money into different financial products with the hope of receiving a return, such as stocks, bonds, mutual funds, or real estate. Rental income, dividends, interest, or capital growth are all possible ways to get a return on your investment.

Investments are essential because they enable people to increase their wealth beyond what they could do with only savings. People may benefit from the power of compound interest over a longer time by investing. For instance, stock market investments may provide large returns over time. Long-term returns in the stock market typically average 10% annually, which is much greater than interest rates on savings accounts.

Additionally, investing may assist people in achieving financial independence and a comfortable retirement. Individuals may create a portfolio that produces enough money to satisfy their costs without having to engage with careful planning and investing. This may provide monetary independence and stability, enabling people to follow their hobbies and passions without worrying about their financial situation.

Saving and investing may aid people in taking advantage of chances in addition to supplying stability and security in their financial situation. Being able to seize opportunities, like investing in a potential business or buying a house at a bargain price, depends on having a healthy savings account and investment portfolio.

Saving money and making investments may also provide people a feeling of satisfaction and financial security. People might feel more in control of their life and more empowered by taking charge of their financial destiny. They may rest easy knowing they have a strategy in place to meet their financial objectives and create a stable future for their children and themselves.

While saving helps people accumulate a cash reserve to cover their immediate and short-term requirements, investing is essential for long-term wealth growth. People may attain their financial objectives, amass wealth, and become financially independent by setting aside money on a regular basis and investing it in different financial products. Saving and investing are not only about acquiring cash; they also help people feel secure and free financially, enabling them to follow their interests and have fulfilling lives.

The Role of Entrepreneurship in Achieving Prosperity

Entrepreneurship has always been essential to the expansion and development of economies. Innovation, job creation, and wealth development are all driven by entrepreneurs. By bringing new goods, services, and business methods, they see possibilities, take calculated risks, and provide value for society. They aid in the expansion of economies and the development of wealth in this manner.

Since entrepreneurship promotes economic development and employment creation, it is crucial for reaching prosperity. Entrepreneurs who launch new firms provide employment and stimulate the economy. This then opens doors for more company owners to launch new ventures, resulting in further job creation and economic expansion. This positive feedback loop is essential for long-term economic success.

Entrepreneurship encourages innovation, which furthers wealth. Entrepreneurs have a natural tendency to see issues and create ways to fix them. The cornerstone of innovation is this process of recognizing issues and coming up with solutions. Entrepreneurs develop new goods and services or enhance those that already exist, which stimulates economic development and benefits society.

Additionally, entrepreneurship encourages competition, which is essential for wealth and economic progress. New goods, services, and business concepts are all introduced when entrepreneurs launch new companies. As a result, markets become more effective, prices decline, and goods and services improve in quality. Competition also motivates company owners to continuously innovate and enhance their operations, which promotes wealth and economic progress.

Social mobility is another way that entrepreneurship helps to create wealth. Entrepreneurs come from many walks of life, and they open doors for people from all backgrounds to succeed. This is crucial, particularly in poorer nations where social mobility is often constrained. People may build their own riches and enhance their lives via entrepreneurship.

Additionally, entrepreneurship supports regional growth, which is essential for reaching wealth. Entrepreneurs who launch new enterprises stimulate the economy in their communities. As a result, the business's economic gains spread to other economic sectors, creating a multiplier effect. This in turn generates new employment and business possibilities in the area, enhancing the general wealth of the neighborhood.

But becoming an entrepreneur can also be a dangerous and difficult job. Entrepreneurs often have to overcome considerable challenges such restricted access to financing, bureaucratic restrictions, and fierce market rivalry. As a result, it is critical that politicians establish an environment that encourages and promotes entrepreneurship.

By facilitating access to capital, easing regulatory constraints, and encouraging innovation, policymakers may boost entrepreneurship. They may also support entrepreneurship education and training to provide prospective company owners the information and abilities they need to launch and expand prosperous enterprises. They may also develop enabling environments that encourage entrepreneur networking, cooperation, and information exchange.

In order to flourish, entrepreneurship is essential. It supports innovation, competitiveness, social mobility, and regional development while fostering economic growth and job creation. In order to encourage and promote entrepreneurship, authorities must provide an enabling environment. They may encourage economic expansion, job development, and general prosperity by doing this.

Chapter 5
Passion & Purpose

The Importance of Finding Your Passion and Purpose for Achieving Prosperity

Finding your passion and purpose in life is crucial for obtaining prosperity. In the long term, higher outcomes and success may result from putting more time and effort into a task that you genuinely enjoy. You can find direction, motivation, and a sense of fulfillment from having a clear sense of purpose, all of which can enhance your general wellbeing.

Passion and purpose are connected ideas, and depending on one's viewpoint, they can be characterized in several ways. A great desire or enthusiasm for anything is referred to as having passion, whereas the motivation or purpose behind one's actions or decisions is referred to as having purpose. These two come together to form a potent force that can assist you in realizing your ambitions.

Finding your passion and purpose can provide you a strong sense of direction in life, which is one of the key advantages. You are more likely to set and work toward particular goals when you are clear on what you want to accomplish and why. By doing so, you may keep your attention on what really matters while avoiding distractions. As you have a clearer grasp of what is important to you, you can make better decisions about your work, relationships, and other aspects of your life when you have a purpose in mind.

Having more motivation and inventiveness is another benefit of following your passion and purpose. You are more likely to enjoy the process of learning, discovering, and producing when you are enthusiastic about something. You may enter a state of flow as a result, in which you are totally focused on your job and more likely to come up with novel ideas and answers. A sense of meaning and significance that comes from having a clear mission may be extremely motivating and exhilarating.

Finding your passion and purpose can result in increased life satisfaction and pleasure in addition to these advantages. You are more likely to feel content and joyful when you are engaged in work that you enjoy and that supports your values and objectives. Your overall health and life quality may be enhanced by this. In contrast, if you are not following your passion and purpose, you could feel dissatisfied or stuck, which can cause discontent and unpleasant feelings.

Finding your passion and purpose is crucial to obtaining prosperity since it can assist you in building a fruitful and prosperous career. You are more likely to succeed in what you do because you are naturally motivated to study and advance your skills when you are doing something you love. This may result in more prospects for career progression, a higher income, and an all-around more satisfying job. Beyond financial success, pursuing your passion and purpose increases your chances of having a positive impact on both your career and the lives of others, which can give you a sense of fulfillment and meaning.

In conclusion, discovering your passion and purpose in life is essential for success. You are more likely to achieve your goals and experience better contentment and happiness in life when you have a clear sense of direction, motivation, and fulfillment. Following your passion and purpose can result in a rewarding job that allows you to make a difference in the world. To ensure that your work and personal choices are in line with your interests, values, and ambitions, it is crucial to take the time to investigate them.

The Role of Resilience in Achieving Prosperity

Resilience is the capacity to adjust to difficulties, get beyond roadblocks, and keep a good attitude despite hardship. It is a crucial quality that is necessary for reaching prosperity, both personally and professionally. People do not naturally possess resilience; rather, it is a skill that can be acquired with dedication and practice. We shall discuss the significance of resilience in reaching prosperity below.

First and foremost, having resilience is crucial for overcoming challenges and disappointments. There will always be challenges to overcome, no matter how well we arrange our lives or our jobs. These challenges could be anything from a botched project to a tragic personal experience. By giving us the willpower and will to press on despite these setbacks, resilience aids in our ability to get over them. It enables us to grow and develop by assisting us in learning from our errors. When faced with difficulty, if we lack resilience, we are more prone to feel overwhelmed and give up.

Second, resilience is necessary to keep a cheerful viewpoint. Even when things are not going well, we need to keep an optimistic mindset if we want to be prosperous. This optimism enables us to maintain our motivation, perceive chances where others only see difficulties, and keep our goals in mind. By giving us the tenacity and resolve to persist even in the face of overwhelming odds, resilience enables us to uphold this positive.

Thirdly, acquiring new abilities and competencies requires resilience. We need to be open to learning new things and gaining new abilities if we want to succeed. To do this, we must venture outside of our comfort zones and take calculated risks. This is made possible by resilience, which gives us the self-assurance and bravery to take these risks. It enables us to face our fears and challenge ourselves.

Fourth, developing successful relationships requires resilience. Building solid relationships with other people is also a key component of prosperity, in addition to financial success. By enabling us to empathize with people, communicate clearly, and establish trust, resilience aids in this process. It assists us in navigating challenging circumstances and establishing solid, long-lasting bonds that can stand the test of time.

Last but not least, resilience is critical to preserving our bodily and mental wellbeing. We must keep up our physical and mental health in order to flourish. This is made possible through resilience, which gives us the power and drive to look after ourselves. It encourages us to establish healthy routines, such as consistent exercise and nutritious eating, and to set aside time for self-care and renewal.

Resilience is crucial for gaining prosperity, to sum up. It supports our ability to overcome challenges, keep an optimistic outlook, acquire new abilities, forge solid bonds with others, and preserve both our physical and mental health. Resilience is a skill that can be learned through practice and dedication, even if it is not something that people are born with. We can accomplish the success and prosperity we seek in both our personal and professional lives by putting our efforts toward strengthening our resilience.

Importance of Work-Life Balance in Achieving Prosperity

For people who want to live prosperous lives, finding a balance between their work and personal lives is essential. More than only financial achievement, prosperity also includes the state of being healthy physically, emotionally, and mentally. Achieving a work-life balance allows a person to manage their obligations at work and in their personal lives, which is crucial for long-term success. As a result, they are more likely to experience more prosperity.

It is simple to become caught up in a loop of work without taking the time to focus on other aspects of life in today's fast-paced world with its high job expectations. Although employment is necessary to support a living, it shouldn't come at the expense of a person's wellbeing. Burnout, stress, and anxiety are consequences of failing to maintain a healthy work-life balance, and they can eventually prevent someone from becoming prosperous.

Maintaining good physical health is the first method that establishing work-life balance is crucial for prosperity. Being physically well is important for maintaining high levels of productivity at work. According to studies, those who place a high priority on exercise and a healthy diet are more productive and motivated at work. Additionally, they have fewer health problems, which results in less time away from work and better job performance. A good diet, frequent exercise, and a balanced lifestyle that promotes restful sleep all contribute to maintaining physical well-being and are essential for reaching success.

Maintaining a healthy balance between work and life is also crucial for mental and emotional health. Burnout, stress, and anxiety can result from neglecting one's emotional and mental health, which can ultimately affect one's capacity for productive work. Spending time doing stress-relieving activities, such as spending time with loved ones, engaging in hobbies, or practicing mindfulness, can greatly enhance emotional and mental wellbeing. Better job satisfaction and higher productivity are eventually linked to better emotional and mental health, which leads to affluence.

Work-life harmony is also essential for preserving positive bonds with family members. Failure to prioritize family relationships can result in strained bonds, which can harm a person's general wellbeing. A sense of belonging and support from family and friends is crucial for one's emotional and mental health. Relationships and general well-being can be greatly enhanced by participating in activities with loved ones, such as taking a vacation, attending social events, or spending quality time together.

Finding a work-life balance also enables personal development. Experiential learning and personal development can occur when people participate in hobbies, travel, and other extracurricular activities. Increased confidence, greater work performance, and better decision-making skills can all contribute to personal growth and development, which in turn can lead to financial success.

Finally, prosperity can only be attained by striking a balance between work and personal life. Improved physical, emotional, and mental health, wholesome connections with loved ones, and personal growth and development are all benefits of work-life balance. Without spending the time to concentrate on these areas, it is simple to become overwhelmed by work and fall short of long-term success. Therefore, in order to flourish in all spheres of life, people must prioritize work- life balance.

The Power of Delegation and Outsourcing in Achieving Prosperity

Businesses can use outsourcing and delegation as two effective strategies to grow. While outsourcing entails using external contractors or businesses to carry out work or supply services, delegation entails giving other employees within the corporation specific roles and duties. Both approaches have the potential to significantly boost overall profitability while promoting growth and productivity.

Businesses can take use of the skills and talents of their staff by delegating. Businesses may guarantee that work is executed more effectively and efficiently by distributing responsibilities to individuals who are most suited for them. For business owners and managers, delegation helps free up time and resources so they may concentrate on more strategic initiatives and higher-level decision-making.

Delegation promotes a sense of ownership and accountability among employees, which is one of its main advantages. People tend to be more committed in their work and are more inclined to take pride in their results when they are given greater freedom and responsibility. Higher levels of employee engagement, work happiness, and general performance may result from this.

On the other side, outsourcing enables organizations to access specialized knowledge and resources that they might not otherwise have. For instance, a business may contract with a third party service to handle its accounting or IT needs, which can lower expenses and boost productivity. By utilizing the skills of outside partners, outsourcing can also assist organizations in gaining access to new markets and prospects.

The ability to concentrate on core expertise is one of outsourcing's largest benefits. Businesses can free up time and resources to concentrate on what they do best by outsourcing non-core operations. By enabling organizations to set themselves apart from their rivals, this can enhance overall competitiveness and profitability.

Outsourcing also has the potential to improve risk management for firms. Businesses might avoid the expenses and liabilities involved with maintaining in-house capabilities, for instance, by outsourcing specific operations.

By doing so, you may be able to lower your overall risk exposure and boost your financial success.

It's crucial to remember that outsourcing and delegating are not without their difficulties. To guarantee that both objectives are carried out successfully, careful planning and administration are necessary. Businesses must make sure, for instance, that they assign jobs to workers who are competent and able to complete them properly. To make sure that assigned activities are executed on schedule and to the acceptable standard, they must also establish clear channels of communication and accountability.

Similarly, companies must exercise caution when choosing outsourcing partners to make sure they are dependable, qualified, and compatible with their strategic goals. Additionally, they must set up explicit contracts and service level agreements to guarantee that functions that are outsourced are completed to the requisite standard and on time.

Finally, delegating and outsourcing are effective strategies that companies can utilize to grow. Businesses can increase efficiency, productivity, and overall performance by giving tasks and responsibilities to staff. Businesses can access specialized resources, cut expenses, and better manage risks by outsourcing non- core operations to outside partners. Businesses must take care to develop and manage these tactics well, as well as provide open channels of communication and responsibility, if they are to be successful. Businesses can achieve long-term growth and profitability by doing this and utilizing the full potential of delegating and outsourcing.

The Role of Time Management in Achieving Prosperity

Time is a limited resource that cannot be replaced and is a major factor in determining our level of success and prosperity. Effective time management is a crucial skill for reaching prosperity since it is a limited resource that we cannot restore once it is used up.

The art of effectively allocating time to accomplish tasks and reach goals is known as time management. Making the most of the time that is available requires prioritizing tasks, planning activities, and scheduling them. There are many advantages to time management, and it can aid people in realizing their potential and achieving their goals.

By raising productivity, time management is one of the main ways it helps people become prosperous. We can do more work in less time when we successfully manage our time. As a result, there is an uptick in efficiency and effectiveness, which boosts output and success levels. In addition to reducing distractions and focusing on the most important activities, time management also helps people be more productive.

Managing your time well is essential for lowering stress. We may approach our work with confidence and without concern when we have a strategy for our time and are aware of the things we must complete. This results in an improved mental state and a more optimistic attitude on life, both of which are necessary for obtaining prosperity.

Effective time management not only lowers stress levels but also aids people in maintaining a positive work-life balance. Effective time management can be difficult given the demands of both job and personal life. To guarantee that we have enough time for work, family, and leisure activities, we can prioritize our tasks and set aside time for each. This supports people in maintaining a prosperous lifestyle, which is essential for health.

Through the encouragement of self-control and discipline, time management also helps to prosperity. Effective time management teaches us to prioritize our tasks and manage our time accordingly. This calls for self-control and discipline, two attributes necessary for success. People can cultivate these traits and use them in other aspects of their lives by engaging in time management practices, which will increase their prosperity.

People who manage their time well also develop better habits. When we efficiently manage our time, we establish a routine that helps us to do activities reliably. This practice turns into a habit that we can employ to consistently accomplish our objectives. When we efficiently manage our time, we establish a routine that allows us to regularly finish our tasks. This practice develops into a habit that helps us regularly accomplish our objectives. We can develop healthy habits that improve our overall prosperity, such as setting aside time each day to exercise or meditate.

Finally, time management enables people to maximize their available resources. We also have limited amounts of energy, attention, and resources in addition to time. We may better allocate these resources and increase our prosperity by practicing excellent time management. We can use our resources more efficiently and get greater results, for instance, by scheduling difficult work for when we are most alert.

In a nutshell, effective time management is a key skill for success. It aids people in improving their productivity, lowering their stress levels, preserving a positive work-life balance, encouraging self-control and discipline, forming better routines, and making the most of their available resources. Planning, prioritizing, and discipline are necessary for effective time management, but the rewards are well worth the effort. People can attain their objectives and realize their full potential by becoming adept at time management, which will result in a prosperous and fulfilling life.

Chapter 6
Your Network

The Importance of Surrounding Yourself with Positive and Supportive People for Achieving Prosperity

Prosperity is a difficult and comprehensive process that depends on a variety of elements, including education, talent, labor, and faith. Your social circle, however, is one of the most important variables that might affect your performance. The saying "you are the average of the five people you spend the most time with" is frequently used. Therefore, a huge impact on your success can be had by surrounding oneself with positive and encouraging people.

Being surrounded by uplifting and encouraging individuals can help you succeed for a number of reasons. First of all, cheerful people frequently have a more upbeat attitude on life, which is spreadable. Being around people who are optimistic about life might influence you and help you develop a more optimistic outlook on life. This can be especially useful when dealing with obstacles or setbacks since a positive outlook can help you stay inspired and committed to your objectives.

Second, you can get the emotional support and useful assistance you need from helpful others to accomplish your goals. Having a support network may be very beneficial, whether it is for listening, advice, or assistance with particular chores. This is crucial when attempting to become prosperous because doing so frequently entails taking chances and venturing outside of your comfort zone. Having individuals who support and believe in you might offer you the assurance and motivation you need to take such actions.

Thirdly, positive and encouraging people can act as inspiration and role models. Being in the presence of successful and prosperous people can inspire you to pursue similar objectives. You can get insightful knowledge and practical suggestions that you can use to your own life by observing the habits, attitudes, and behaviors that have contributed to the success of others.

On the other hand, it might be harmful to your prosperity to be surrounded by unfavorable and unsupportive individuals. Pessimistic outlooks on life are a hallmark of negative people, and they may be tiring and demotivating. They might also dissuade you from taking chances or achieving your objectives if they don't think you can accomplish it or if they themselves are terrified of failing. Being around by those who frequently criticize or minimize you can also undermine your self-esteem and undermine your sense of self-worth, making it more difficult for you to take the necessary actions to achieve prosperity.

Negative people can also be a source of drama and diversion, which can consume your time and energy. Dealing with the issues or negativity of others can be draining and leave you with less time and mental room to concentrate on your own objectives. Additionally, it may foster an environment that is poisonous and inhibits creativity and innovation, making it more difficult for you to come up with fresh concepts and solutions.

Therefore, it is essential to surround yourself with positive and encouraging individuals if you want to flourish. Positive people can serve as role models, sources of inspiration, and emotional and practical assistance. They can also help you adopt a more positive attitude on life. However, negative and unhelpful people can be taxing, distracting, and demotivating, which will make it more difficult for you to accomplish your objectives. As a result, it's crucial to choose your friends carefully and spend time with those who will help you on your path to financial success.

The Power of Giving Back to Society of Achieving Prosperity

Giving back to society has a powerful impact that cannot be underestimated. Giving back has been shown to have a positive contagious impact that can ultimately result in success for both the person and society as a whole. Giving back has several advantages, such as personal development, a sense of fulfillment, and even financial success.

Giving back has several advantages, but one of the biggest is personal development. When people volunteer in their communities, they are exposed to fresh ideas and viewpoints that can challenge their assumptions and widen their views.

People may experience personal growth and development as a result of this as they become more conscious of their own values, beliefs, and objectives. People can develop a feeling of purpose and meaning in their life by volunteering or making donations to groups that share their values. This can ultimately result in greater pleasure and contentment.

Giving back can result in both personal development and financial prosperity. Many successful business owners and executives have made charity initiatives the foundation of their success. These people have developed enduring connections with their clients and stakeholders by giving back to their communities and championing philanthropic causes, which has eventually increased company success. According to a Cone Communications study, 91% of consumers are more willing to support a brand that advocates for social or environmental causes.

Giving back to society can also contribute to its prosperity. The most urgent issues facing society today, such as poverty, inequality, and climate change, can be addressed by people and organizations who invest in social and environmental causes. Along with higher economic growth and wealth, this may result in greater social stability and cohesion. For instance, funding education and training initiatives can help people acquire the abilities and information required to excel in the workforce, which can ultimately result in greater economic success for both the person and the larger society.

And finally, helping others can contribute to a society that is more egalitarian and just. Individuals and organizations can help level the playing field for marginalized communities and encourage greater social participation by supporting activities that advance social justice and equality. This may result in a more lively and diversified society where everyone has the chance to prosper. Giving back can ultimately result in a more democratic and accountable society by fostering increased civic involvement and participation.

In a nutshell, it is evident that contributing to society can help people succeed. Individuals and groups can foster personal development, financial success, and social and economic prosperity through supporting social and environmental issues. Additionally, we may contribute to the development of a more fair and equitable society where everyone has the chance to prosper by supporting initiatives that advance social justice and equality. Giving back to society is, in the end, both the morally correct thing to do and the practical thing to do for both people and society at large.

How to Stay Motivated and Focused on Your Prosperity Goals

Setting prosperous objectives is a crucial step on the road to success. However, maintaining motivation and concentration on these objectives can be difficult, particularly when encountering setbacks and diversions. The good news is that you can stay on track and accomplish your prosperity goals if you adopt the proper attitude and methods. The following advice can help you stay inspired and committed to your financial goals.

<u>Clarify your financial objectives.</u> Setting precise definitions for your prosperity goals is the first step in maintaining motivation and focus. With a goal that is well defined, it is simpler to imagine your desired outcome and maintain concentration. Make sure your prosperity goals are SMART (specific, measurable, attainable, relevant, and time-bound) as you are defining them. This will enable you to monitor your progress and make any necessary corrections.

<u>Divide up your objectives into manageable tasks.</u> Once your prosperity objectives have been established, divide them up into manageable activities. This will aid in keeping you motivated and preventing feelings of overload.

You can focus on one item at a time by making a daily, weekly, or monthly to-do list.

Make a plan and follow it. Making a strategy is essential to attaining your financial objectives. A strategy enables you to stay organized, monitor your advancement, and change your course of action as necessary. Think about your resources, timeframe, priorities, and any obstacles as you draft your plan. You can keep on track and stay focused on your objectives with the aid of a plan.

Remain upbeat and concentrated. Maintaining motivation requires remaining upbeat and concentrated. Keep your attention on the progress you are making and enjoy minor victories along the way. It is crucial to keep in mind that obstacles and problems will inevitably arise along the way, but they shouldn't stop you from reaching your objectives. Make the most of setbacks to develop and learn.

Be in the company of uplifting individuals. To stay motivated and engaged, it's essential to surround yourself with positive individuals. When you face difficulties, positive individuals will cheer you on and support you. They will also celebrate your accomplishments. On the other hand, negative people can depress you and sap your strength. Pick your friends and coworkers carefully.

Take motivation and inspiration from other people. It might be a great way to keep motivated and inspired to pursue your financial goals. You can follow successful people on social media, read books, listen to podcasts, and attend seminars or conferences, or all of the above. Take advice from their mistakes and be inspired by their tales to keep motivated.

<u>Reward your accomplishments with yourself.</u> It's a terrific method to keep oneself focused and motivated to reward you for accomplishments. Take some time to rejoice and treat yourself when you reach a goal. This could be as simple as treating yourself to your favorite dinner or purchasing a long-desired item. Rewarding yourself keeps you motivated and committed to your objectives.

In the long run, maintaining motivation and a laser-like concentration on your financial objectives is crucial for success in life. Some advice that can help you stay motivated and focused includes clearly defining your goals, breaking them down into smaller tasks, developing a plan, remaining positive and focused, surrounding yourself with positive people, finding inspiration and motivation from others, and rewarding yourself for accomplishments. Keep in mind that reaching your prosperity objectives will require time, patience, and perseverance, but with the correct attitude and skills, you may succeed and lead the life you want.

The Role of Mentors and Coaches in Achieving Prosperity

In order for people to flourish in both their personal and professional life, mentors and coaches are essential. The ability to achieve financial security, personal development, and a sense of fulfillment is referred to as prosperity in this context. People can realize their potential, get over challenges, and move closer to their objectives with the help and support of mentors and coaches.

Individuals who have already found success in a given sector and are eager to impart their wisdom to others are known as mentors. They serve as role models, providing counsel and direction on how to overcome the difficulties encountered when pursuing a certain career route. A mentor can offer helpful industry insights, support in locating growth possibilities, and advice on how to get beyond challenges. For instance, a mentor in the finance sector could offer advice on how to manage the complexity of the stock market or create a profitable portfolio.

On the other side, coaches are people who focus on assisting others in acquiring the abilities and perspective required to accomplish their goals. Instead of needing to be experts in a particular industry like mentors do, coaches are trained to offer advice and support for both professional and personal development. In order to assist people in overcoming limiting beliefs, acquiring new abilities, and moving closer to their objectives, they employ a number of tools and strategies. An individual might receive assistance from a life coach, for instance, in setting goals and developing a strategy to reach them.

Together, mentors and coaches offer a potent mix of support and direction that can aid people in achieving prosperity. Some of the ways they can help someone succeed are as follows:

They offer direction and assistance. Mentors and coaches offer direction and assistance, assisting people in navigating the difficulties and uncertainties encountered when pursuing their goals. They can provide knowledge about the market or area of interest, assist in locating development potential, and offer suggestions on how to do better.

They aid in determining one's assets and shortcomings. Individuals can design a strategy to build on their talents and address their flaws with the assistance of mentors and coaches who can help them recognize their strengths and limitations. This can give a sense of direction and boost confidence.

They provide responsibility. Mentors and coaches can assist people in maintaining accountability for their objectives and deeds. In spite of obstacles or setbacks, this can help people stay dedicated to their objectives and stay focused.

They inspire: Mentors and coaches may inspire and motivate people, assisting them in staying inspired and motivated to accomplish their goals. This is particularly crucial when people are faced with problems that may otherwise lead them to give up in uncertain situations.

They promote a sense of belonging. People can connect with others who share their interests and ambitions with the support of mentors and coaches. Taken differently, this can foster a sense of belonging and support, keeping people inspired and engaged.

In conclusion, it is impossible to emphasize the importance of mentors and coaches in reaching prosperity. They offer crucial direction, encouragement, accountability, and motivation, assisting people in realizing their full potential, overcoming challenges, and moving closer to their objectives. A mentor or coach can be a valuable resource for success, whether a person is pursuing a certain job path or looking for personal fulfillment.

Chapter 7
Goals

The Importance of Setting Realistic and Achievable Goals for Prosperity

Setting goals is a vital part of life that motivates us to fulfill our desires. Our efforts may be prioritized with the aid of goals, which can also provide us with a feeling of direction, purpose, and fulfillment. Setting unattainable or unreasonable objectives, however, can be discouraging and prevent us from achieving our aspirations. In order to achieve success, it is crucial to create goals that are both attainable and practical.

The state of being successful or thriving in both the financial and social spheres is frequently used to characterize prosperity. Despite the fact that everyone's concept of prosperity may differ, it often entails having access to enough resources to meet one's necessities, living a life of high quality, and finding personal fulfillment. Here are some reasons why establishing attainable objectives is essential for achieving prosperity:

Drive and Concentration

Setting attainable goals will keep you motivated and committed to your goals. When your ambitions are overly ambitious, you could experience overwhelm and not know where to begin. Procrastination, tension, and even failure may result from this. Setting reasonable objectives that are compatible with your present skills and resources, on the other hand, might help you feel in charge and oriented. This, in turn, inspires you to act and move closer to your objectives.

Measurable Development

Setting attainable objectives enables you to track your development and gauge your success. This is crucial since it increases your confidence and gives you a sense of success. You may discover areas that require development and change your goals as necessary by tracking your progress. In this manner, you can proceed and continue down the path to success.

Resilience and Flexibility

Being adaptive and resilient is also a must for setting realistic and doable objectives. Because life is erratic, unforeseen difficulties can occur at any time. Setting excessively inflexible or unattainable objectives might make it difficult to adjust to changing circumstances or setbacks. However, you may be more adaptable and change your plans as necessary when you create attainable objectives. This enables you to develop resilience and get past setbacks.

<u>Sustainable Development</u>

You may move steadily toward riches by setting attainable objectives. Setting too ambitious objectives might lead to instant success but difficulty maintaining them over time. Burnout, dissatisfaction, and even setbacks may result from this. However, you can advance consistently and sustainably when you set attainable objectives. You may preserve your successes in this manner and prosper over the long term.

Therefore, gaining success depends on having objectives that are both attainable and practical. Setting objectives that are in line with your present talents and resources may help you stay motivated, track your progress, adjust to changing circumstances, and achieve sustainable development, whether you want to establish a business, save for retirement, or raise your social standing. Setting attainable objectives can help you reach your full potential and find the riches you seek.

How To Track Your Progress Towards Achieving Prosperity

Many individuals aspire to achieve prosperity in their lives. It's a condition in which one has access to adequate chances and resources to have a happy existence. The road to success can be difficult, though, so it's crucial to have a tool to monitor your progress. Here are some guidelines for monitoring your development toward financial prosperity.

Establish precise objectives.

Setting specific goals is the first step to achieving riches. Set measurable objectives to help you reach your definition of prosperity. These objectives must be clear, quantifiable, doable, timely, and relevant. For instance, if financial security is your definition of success, you can establish a goal to save a certain amount of money each month or to settle all of your bills by a certain date.

Keep an eye on your money.

Your financial situation is crucial to obtaining prosperity. To make sure you are moving closer to your financial objectives, you need to keep track of your earnings, outgoing costs, and investment activity. Utilize a budgeting tool to keep tabs on your spending, and check in frequently to see how your assets are doing.

Analyze the development of your career.

Another important component of prospering is your career. Regularly evaluate your professional development to see if you are on the right path to reaching your objectives. To determine where you need to improve, evaluate your performance, abilities, and accomplishments. To improve your abilities and expertise, think about enrolling in classes or attending seminars.

Monitor your own development.

Prosperity requires constant personal development. By monitoring your personal development objectives, you can gauge your own improvement. Analyze your leadership potential, communication prowess, and emotional intelligence. To improve these talents, think about enrolling in classes or attending seminars.

Maintain an optimistic outlook.

When measuring your progress towards financial prosperity, it's crucial to keep an optimistic outlook. Keep in mind that failure and setbacks are necessary steps on the path to success. Learn from your errors and take advantage of the chance to advance. Honor your accomplishments, no matter how little they may be.

Receive criticism

Tracking your development toward success requires you to actively seek feedback. To assess your development, get comments from your peers, mentors, or coaches. To assist you in achieving your objectives, think about joining a mastermind group or looking for a mentor.

Honor your accomplishments.

Salute your progress and accomplishments. Set goals, and when you achieve them, rejoice. Reward yourself for your effort and hard work. Celebrating your accomplishments might inspire you to keep moving forward in the direction of financial prosperity.

Adapt your strategy.

Finally, in order to make sure that you are moving toward financial prosperity, it is critical to frequently modify your strategy. Regularly review your objectives and gauge your success. Make changes to your strategy if you realize that you are not progressing as expected. It's important to keep in mind that becoming prosperous is a journey and that you must be adaptive and flexible along the way.

Finally, success depends on keeping track of your progress toward financial achievement. Establish specific objectives, keep an eye on your money, evaluate your career's advancement, keep tabs on your personal development, keep an optimistic outlook, ask for input, acknowledge your accomplishments, and continually revise your strategy. Keep in mind that obtaining success is a journey that calls for commitment, toil, and a readiness to learn and develop. With the help of these suggestions, you may continue working toward your objectives and leading a successful life.

The Power of Accountability in Achieving Prosperity

Accountability is essential for achieving prosperity on both a personal and societal level. It refers to a person's or an organization's responsibility for their choices and actions, as well as their commitment to be open and accountable for the results. When people and organizations accept responsibility, they are better equipped to reach their objectives because they can monitor their progress, spot opportunities for improvement, and respond appropriately when necessary. Below, we'll examine the role that responsibility plays in generating prosperity and the ways in which it may help people, businesses, and society at large.

First off, responsibility is important for both personal development and progress. People are better able to see their strengths, limitations, and opportunities for progress when they accept responsibility for their actions and decisions. They can create doable objectives, monitor their progress, and change course as necessary because they are self-aware. For instance, if someone is aiming to lose weight, they may decide to commit to exercising daily for 30 minutes and monitor their results with a fitness app. They are more likely to continue with their goal and get the result they want if they are responsible for themselves.

Accountability has advantages for both individuals and businesses. Organizations that embrace accountability become more open and reliable, which can boost customer satisfaction and loyalty. Organizations may evaluate their performance and pinpoint areas for growth by establishing clear goals and success criteria. As a result, they are able to continually enhance their goods and services and make data-driven decisions. For instance, a business could decide to measure its progress toward a 10% carbon footprint reduction objective using sustainability indicators. They may show their commitment to sustainability and draw in environmentally concerned customers by being accountable to their stakeholders.

Additionally, accountability can spur cooperation and creativity. When people and organizations are held accountable for their actions, they are more inclined to look for fresh views and ideas as well as work together to accomplish their objectives. As a result of the variety of viewpoints and ideas that are presented, this may result in more creative and inventive solutions. For instance, a team developing a new product may ask stakeholders from various departments or outside partners for input and considerations, which they then incorporate into their design. They may provide a product that satisfies their demands and surpasses their expectations by being accountable to their consumers and stakeholders.

Accountability may also encourage moral conduct and societal responsibility. People and organizations are more likely to behave responsibly and ethically when they are held accountable for their activities. As students consider how their choices may affect others and the environment, this may have a positive social and environmental impact. For instance, a business could decide to cooperate with suppliers to acquire all of its raw materials from sustainable sources. They may demonstrate their dedication to moral and sustainable practices and encourage others to follow suit by being accountable to their stakeholders.

Last but not least, accountability may enhance our common prosperity. Together, people and groups may achieve successful social and economic results for themselves, their communities, and their worlds. They may develop trust, encourage cooperation, and have a bigger effect by being accountable to one another. For instance, a network of company owners may be established to pool resources and knowledge and assist one another in expanding their enterprises. They may build a healthy ecosystem of innovation and entrepreneurship and contribute to the regional economy by holding one another responsible.

In conclusion, responsibility is a potent instrument for both personal and societal prosperity. It encourages individual development, corporate performance, creativity and teamwork, moral conduct and social responsibility, and societal progress. Individuals and organizations may reach their full potential and produce beneficial results for both themselves and their communities by embracing responsibility. It is therefore crucial.

The Importance of Celebrating Your Achievements Along the Way

The idea of accountability is accepting accountability for one's deeds, choices, and results. It is crucial for reaching prosperity in any area, whether it is social, professional, or personal. Accountability is essential for ensuring that objectives are met, agreements are kept, and success-oriented steps are taken. The strength of accountability resides in its capacity to foster a sense of ownership, dedication, and responsibility toward a common objective, which eventually results in success.

Setting specific, measurable objectives is the first step in achieving success through responsibility. Setting goals gives you direction and a point of concentration as you work toward your goal. Individuals and organizations can identify the necessary activities and resources to attain their goals when they have clear and defined goals. To guarantee that the goals are attained, a system of accountability must be put in place in addition to goal planning. Roles and duties must be established, deadlines must be defined, and progress must be tracked.

Accountability encourages a culture of ownership, accountability, and dedication to attaining objectives. As people and organizations are held accountable for their deeds and choices, it promotes a sense of trust and dependability. Accountability helps people and organizations develop and improve over time by learning from their errors and failures. Accountability then turns into a potent instrument for creating wealth.

In every company, whether it be a small firm or a major enterprise, accountability is crucial. Accountability means ensuring that workers are held accountable for their actions and provides the desired results. Additionally, it aids in the detection and prevention of fraud, misconduct, and other unethical activities. Accountability in this way fosters fairness and openness, both of which are essential for gaining the respect and confidence of stakeholders.

Achieving success on a communal level requires accountability as well. Governments and public organizations are in charge of offering residents fundamental services, including infrastructure, healthcare, and education. Since taxpayers are paying for these services, it is crucial to make sure they are provided successfully and efficiently. Public institutions must be held accountable to the citizens they serve through accountability procedures, including audits, public hearings, and citizen input.

Even in the private sector, accountability is effective. Businesses with a focus on accountability have a greater chance of long-term success. Accountability guarantees that companies are accountable for their effects on society, the environment, and stakeholders. Additionally, it encourages moral conduct and openness, both of which are essential for establishing a solid reputation and luring clients and investors. Accountability therefore becomes a competitive advantage, allowing companies to grow over the long term.

Accountability is essential to one's personal growth. People are more likely to succeed in their objectives and aspirations if they accept responsibility for their actions and decisions. Accountability encourages people to grow personally by allowing them to learn from their errors and failings. Additionally, it promotes self-discipline, which is necessary for success in any career.

In a variety of industries, including sports, education, and healthcare, the force of accountability can be observed. Athletes are responsible for their performance and conduct both on and off the field in sports. Accountability guarantees athletes' dedication to their training and a sense of responsibility for their actions, which eventually results in success. Accountability in education means ensuring that both students and instructors are held accountable for delivering high-quality instruction. Accountability in healthcare guarantees that people are held accountable for following medical advice and that healthcare personnel are responsible for delivering high-quality care.

In summary, responsibility is a potent instrument for success in any endeavor. It encourages a culture of accountability, ownership, and dedication to a common objective. Accountability ensures that objectives are met, promises are kept, and success is approached. Transparency, fairness, and moral conduct are encouraged, all of which are essential for establishing confidence and trust. Accountability helps people and organizations develop and improve over time by learning from their errors and failures.

How to Turn Failures and Setbacks into Opportunities for Achieving Prosperity

When we experience failures or setbacks, it's easy to become dejected and think we've reached a dead end. But if we have the appropriate attitude and strategy, we may use these challenges as stepping stones to riches. Here are some pointers for accomplishing it:

Change your perspective by viewing failures as a chance for development and learning rather than as a final destination. We have the opportunity to grow from our mistakes, discover fresh perspectives, and sharpen our abilities when we encounter setbacks. Accept the challenge and see it as an opportunity to improve and fortify yourself.

Examine the circumstances: Take a step back and evaluate the circumstances impartially. What happened? What else could you have done? What can you infer about life from this experience? You may better comprehend what transpired and how to prevent making the same errors in the future by critically evaluating the circumstances.

Determine your strong points. There were probably certain areas where you excelled even in the midst of failure. Determine your advantages, and then concentrate on enhancing them. You will be able to move on with increased enthusiasm and confidence as a result of this.

Create an action plan: After you've assessed the circumstances and determined your abilities, create an action plan for the future. Make a schedule for completing your goals and break them down into smaller, more doable actions. As you work towards your desired objective, this will assist you in remaining motivated and focused.

Don't be scared to ask people for advice and assistance when you need it. Getting an outside viewpoint—whether from a mentor, coworker, or friend—can help you discover fresh thoughts and concepts. Additionally, having a support structure in place might give you the inspiration and drive to continue.

Accept creativity: Sometimes thinking outside the box leads to the finest answers. Explore fresh concepts and methods while embracing creativity. You might not have thought of fresh prospects for success previously, but this can help you find them.

Stay tenacious. Failure and setbacks are unavoidable on the path to achievement. But it's crucial to maintain your resolve and keep moving forward. Success frequently comes to those who are prepared to endure difficulties and setbacks.

Self-care is advisable. It's easy to be sucked into the race for success, but it's crucial to look out for yourself along the way. Spend time engaging in hobbies, fitness, and other enjoyable activities. You can prevent burnout and retain a positive attitude by doing this.

While it's crucial to keep your eye on the big picture, it may also be helpful to recognize and celebrate tiny accomplishments along the way to give yourself a much-needed motivational boost. Give yourself credit for the actions you've taken in the direction of accomplishing your goals by acknowledging your progress.

Discover from others: Finally, don't be reluctant to pick up tips from those who have dealt with comparable difficulties. Read books, go to seminars, and look for mentors who can offer support and assistance. By picking up tips from others, you might gain insightful knowledge and steer clear of typical blunders.

In a nutshell, failures and setbacks are necessary components of the path to success. But if we have the appropriate attitude and strategy, we may use these challenges as stepping stones to riches. We can overcome setbacks and accomplish our goals by changing our perspective, assessing the situation, pinpointing our strengths, creating a plan of action, getting feedback and support, embracing creativity, persevering, engaging in self-care, celebrating small victories, and picking up tips from others.

The Role of Perseverance and Grit in Achieving Prosperity

Grit and perseverance are two characteristics necessary for prosperity. They serve as the foundation for success, motivating people to overcome obstacles and push their personal boundaries. Grit is a mix of enthusiasm and tenacity toward long- term goals. Grit is described as the capacity to continue in the face of challenges. These two characteristics go hand in hand, and those who have both are more likely to flourish in all facets of their lives.

Success in every endeavor, whether it be in business, athletics, or academia, requires tenacity and guts. People in business must endure despite difficulties including financial failures, competition, and shifting markets. They must be able to change course as required and keep their attention on long-term objectives. This calls for grit because people need to be passionate about what they do and ready to put in the time and effort required to succeed.

Perseverance and tenacity are crucial for success in athletics. Athletes need to be able to push beyond their physical limitations, put up with demanding training schedules, and recover from setbacks like injuries. They must be able to stay focused and passionate about their sport despite obstacles and defeats. Athletes must be able to persevere through challenging situations and keep their enthusiasm for their sport to do this, which calls for both persistence and grit.

Perseverance and grit are crucial for academic achievement. The ability to endure through a rigorous curriculum, keep their attention on long-term objectives like graduation and a successful job, and bounce back from setbacks like subpar grades or demanding teachers are requirements for college students. They must be able to push themselves beyond their comfort zones and never lose their enthusiasm for learning, despite obstacles and disappointments. Students must be able to persevere through challenging situations and retain their desire to study to do this, which calls for both perseverance and grit.

Gaining success in personal relationships also requires courage and perseverance. People must be willing to persevere through challenging times and keep their focus on long-term objectives like a healthy marriage or family life, since relationships involve effort and attention. They must be able to keep their enthusiasm for their spouse and their family alive in the face of difficulties like conflicts, disappointments, and defeats. Individuals must be able to persevere through challenging situations and keep their love for their relationships, which calls for both persistence and grit.

Perseverance and tenacity are essential for success in all spheres of life. These characteristics increase a person's ability to overcome obstacles, persevere through challenging situations, and keep their attention on long-term objectives. Additionally, they are more likely to continue to be passionate about their jobs, sports, academics, and relationships even in the face of disappointments and losses.

But tenacity and grit by themselves won't bring about riches. Along with having access to opportunities and resources, people must also have other traits like intellect, creativity, and flexibility. Additionally, they must be prepared to take chances, learn from their mistakes, and ask for advice and assistance from others.

Additionally, with experience and effort, tenacity and grit may be acquired over time. People may develop the ability to persevere through challenging situations, keep their attention on long-term objectives, and retain their love for their career, their sport, their academics, and their relationships. This calls for a readiness to learn, develop, and adapt, as well as a willingness to go to others for advice and assistance.

Therefore, tenacity and grit are necessary traits for attaining success in all spheres of life. They are essential for long-term enthusiasm and attention maintenance as well as success in business, sports, academia, and interpersonal relationships. However, these characteristics by themselves are insufficient for obtaining success; people also need to have access to additional characteristics like intellect, creativity, and flexibility.

Chapter 8
Visualization & Manifestation

The Power of Visualization and Manifestation for Achieving Prosperity

In recent years, the idea of visualization and manifestation has become incredibly popular. More people are using these methods to realize their aspirations and accomplish their goals. Wealth, health, relationships, and personal development may all be improved through the use of the powerful skills of visualization and manifestation. Below, we shall examine the effectiveness of visualization and manifestation for creating success.

The act of forming an internal picture of a desired result is known as visualization. It entails seeing your desired outcome in your mind's eye and focusing on that picture with intention and belief. You may use visualization to help you do anything, including enhance your health and create financial abundance. When you imagine, you may manifest your goals by connecting with the energy of the cosmos and using the power of your imagination.

On the other side, manifestation is the process of turning your dreams into reality. It entails making progress toward your objectives while having faith that the universe will assist you in doing so. Faith, intention, and confidence in your capacity to shape your world are necessary for manifestation. You can harness the power of your mind and the cosmos to create the life you want by combining visualization and manifestation. Everything in the cosmos is made of energy, which is where the power of imagination and manifestation comes from. Every thought, feeling, and deed generates a frequency that pulls in other frequencies with a similar frequency. This implies that what you reject endures and what you focus on grows. You boost your vibration and draw good energy into your life by envisioning and achieving your goals.

You must take a few easy actions in order to employ visualization and manifestation to obtain success. You must first determine your objectives and preferences. Getting very clear about your goals and motivations is necessary for this. You may start seeing your goals in great detail after you have clarity on them. This entails seeing your desired outcome in your mind, along with the images, sounds, and emotions that go along with it.

It's crucial to concentrate on the uplifting feelings connected to your goals when you imagine them. This entails being thankful, joyful, and excited as you picture your objectives coming true. You can improve your vibration and draw positive energy into your life by concentrating on pleasant feelings.

It's time to act on your desires once you've visualized them. Setting specific goals and making tiny, regular efforts toward achieving them are required. It's crucial to let go of any uncertainties or concerns that can prevent you from accomplishing your goals and to have faith in the universe to help you.

There are other techniques that can assist you in achieving wealth in addition to visualization and manifestation. These consist of meditation, thankfulness, and inspirational statements. Focusing on what you already have in life and expressing thanks for it are both components of thankfulness. By changing your attention from lack to plenty, you can attract more abundance into your life.

In order to strengthen your beliefs and draw positive energy into your life, you may use positive affirmations, which entail saying kind things to yourself. Positive affirmations contain statements like "I am worthy of prosperity" and "I trust the universe to support me in achieving my desires."

Another effective technique that might assist you in achieving riches is meditation. It entails calming the mind and concentrating on the here and now. By doing so, you may access the power of your subconscious mind and reduce tension and anxiety while also improving clarity and attention.

To ramp it up, it is evident that visualization and manifestation are powerful tools for creating wealth. You can design the life you want by utilizing the power of the cosmos and your imagination. You may begin to employ visualization and manifestation to obtain success in all areas of your life by following the easy methods described in this article. Don't forget to have a good outlook, work consistently toward your objectives, and have faith that the universe will help you succeed.

How to Create a Supportive Environment for Achieving Prosperity

Prosperity may be attained through a complicated and multifaceted process that takes into account a variety of environmental, societal, and psychological aspects. A key stage in this process is creating a supportive atmosphere, which may promote the circumstances needed for success and help people realize their ambitions. Here are some tactics for fostering a welcoming environment that can aid people in achieving success.

Create an optimistic outlook.

Positivity is one of the most important components of a supportive atmosphere. Being prosperous requires having a positive mentality because it enables people to approach opportunities and problems with optimism, confidence, and a willingness to take chances. A variety of techniques, including practicing gratitude, affirmations, visualization, and meditation, can help you develop a good mentality. A happy outlook can also be fostered by surrounding oneself with good people and partaking in positive activities.

Organize a helpful social network.

A supportive social network is an additional essential component of a supportive environment. Joining groups, going to networking events, and doing community service are just a few ways to develop a supportive social network. A helpful social network may offer people possibilities for personal and professional growth, emotional support, and useful advice. A supportive social network can also assist people in finding resources, including employment leads, financial aid, and educational possibilities.

Establish precise objectives.

Setting specific objectives is a crucial first step toward riches. Setting clear objectives enables people to concentrate their efforts and maintain motivation in the face of challenges and disappointments. It is crucial to be precise, quantifiable, and reachable while establishing objectives. To guarantee development and keep momentum, it's also crucial to divide larger goals into smaller, more doable tasks. Individuals may recognize possible obstacles and create tactics to get through them by setting clear goals.

Become growth-oriented.

Another essential component of a favorable atmosphere for obtaining prosperity is a development mentality. A growth mindset is the conviction that one's skills and abilities may be enhanced through effort, commitment, and perseverance. Several tactics, such as accepting challenges, looking for feedback, and learning from mistakes, might help you develop a growth mindset. Additionally, being among people who share a development mentality may support and foster this notion by serving as reinforcement.

Develop a sense of direction.

Another essential component of a conducive atmosphere for prosperity is a sense of purpose. A feeling of purpose is the conviction that one's life has significance and worth and that one's deeds are advancing a greater cause or vision. Finding one's values and interests, making meaningful objectives, and partaking in activities that support one's values and goals are just a few techniques that can help one develop a sense of purpose. Being around others who have the same beliefs and aspirations may also help to strengthen a sense of purpose and offer support and encouragement.

Place self-care first.

Another essential component of a favorable atmosphere for reaching prosperity is self-care. Taking care of one's physical, emotional, and mental health and wellbeing is referred to as practicing self-care. Making self-care a priority may be achieved by a variety of tactics, including obtaining adequate sleep, maintaining a good diet, exercising frequently, and partaking in relaxing and stress-relieving activities. In addition, getting professional assistance when necessary, such as therapy or counseling, may enhance general wellbeing and aid with self-care.

Establish a comfortable physical setting.

As a last step toward success, building a favorable physical environment is also essential. A supportive physical environment may be achieved through a variety of techniques, including setting up a relaxing and practical workstation, setting up one's home for maximum productivity, and surrounding oneself with items and pictures that uplift and inspire. Additionally, maintaining a secure, orderly, and distraction-free physical environment helps encourage a positive workplace.

It can be difficult and demanding to create an atmosphere that promotes prosperity, and it calls for work and dedication. Nevertheless, the advantages of establishing such an atmosphere far outweigh the cost. People may lay the groundwork for a happy and productive life where they are empowered to follow their interests, accomplish their objectives, and give back to their communities by creating a supportive atmosphere.

It is crucial to remember that developing a helpful atmosphere is a continual process that calls for continued effort and adaptability. The environment must alter to accommodate changes in people's situations and objectives. Therefore, it's crucial to continually evaluate the environment and make changes as needed to keep it constructive and functional.

In conclusion, developing an atmosphere that is conducive to prosperity is a complex process that takes into account a variety of psychological, social, and environmental elements. People may construct an environment that enables them to realize their goals and objectives by adopting a positive mentality, forming a supportive social network, establishing clear goals, fostering a growth mindset, prioritizing self-care, and setting up a supportive physical environment. An atmosphere of support may be created by individuals with dedication and effort, laying the groundwork for a happy and productive existence.

The Importance of Giving Yourself Permission to Succeed and Prosper

At first glance, the idea of granting oneself permission to flourish may seem inconsequential or even illogical. After all, effort, skill, and recognition from others are frequently linked to success and fortune. Many individuals, however, are unaware of the important role that their own thinking, beliefs, and attitudes may play in helping them realize their potential and achieve their goals. People may overcome self-doubt, fear of failure, and limiting beliefs and realize their full potential by giving themselves permission to flourish.

What does it mean to grant oneself permission to be successful and prosperous, then? It basically implies having a growth mentality, which is the conviction that one's skills, intelligence, and talents can be improved through commitment and effort. It entails admitting that success is a product of purposeful activity, the ability to learn from failures, and tenacity rather than an elusive or random event. It entails accepting responsibility for one's aspirations and not waiting for approval or validation from others before pursuing them.

Why is this mentality so crucial? First off, it aids in overcoming impostor syndrome and feelings of self-doubt. Many people believe they lack specific traits or qualifications or compare themselves to others who appear to be more successful, which makes them feel undeserving of success or fortune. The more one doubts themselves, the less likely they are to take chances, develop new abilities, or grasp opportunities. However, this mentality is a self-fulfilling prophecy. Giving oneself the go-ahead to achieve recognizes that success is a result of hard work, perseverance, and learning rather than intrinsic skill or good fortune. This kind of thinking can assist people in embracing their potential and skills while overcoming their inner critics.

Second, allowing oneself to achieve can assist people in overcoming their fear of failure. Failure is frequently viewed as an embarrassing or irreparable result that should be avoided at all costs. Failure, however, is a necessary component of development and learning and frequently serves as a springboard for success. By allowing oneself to make errors, one recognizes that failures are not a reflection of one's value or competence but rather a chance to grow. Individuals who adopt this perspective are more likely to take chances, try new things, and innovate than those who play it safe and make do.

Thirdly, allowing oneself to achieve can assist people in overcoming constricting ideas and cultural conditioning. Many individuals are raised with the idea that success is an uncommon and special accomplishment, only available to the fortunate or those with particular advantages. This idea can make people feel defeated or resentful and discourage them from pursuing their goals or realizing their full potential. By allowing oneself to achieve, one disproves this notion and creates new opportunities. One comes to the understanding that success is not a zero-sum game and that no one's achievement detracts from that of others. This kind of thinking can assist people in overcoming the mental obstacles that are holding them back and embracing a more prosperous and upbeat outlook.

And last, allowing oneself to achieve can contribute to a person's sense of fulfillment and purpose. Success and prosperity are frequently linked to tangible or outside benefits, such as income, position, or acclaim. While these benefits might be enjoyable, they are insufficient to bring about contentment or satisfaction that lasts a lifetime. Instead, achieving actual success requires coordinating one's objectives and deeds with one's values, interests, and skills. Giving oneself the go-ahead to achieve helps one develop a feeling of agency and autonomy and recognize that success is a process rather than a destination. This kind of thinking can aid people in discovering meaning and purpose in their careers, interpersonal relationships, and overall lives.

In conclusion, adopting the mentality that one may achieve and prosper is not foolish or self-centered, but strong and essential. People may overcome self- doubt, fear of failure, limiting beliefs, and cultural indoctrination by adopting this mentality, allowing them to realize their full potential.

The Role of Mindfulness and Meditation in Achieving Prosperity

Although the term "prosperity" is sometimes linked to material wealth or success, it really refers to a wide variety of qualities, including contentment, pleasure, and good health. While there are many ways to become wealthy, mindfulness and meditation have become effective techniques for people to use to reach this state of being here, we'll be talking about the benefits of mindfulness and meditation for earning affluence and leading happier lives.

Being present in the moment without passing judgment is the practice of mindfulness. It entails giving your all to the present moment, accepting it as it is rather than attempting to alter it. Meditation is a practice that involves concentrating one's attention on a single thing, idea, or action in order to create an intellectually clear and emotionally peaceful state. Mindfulness is frequently associated with meditation.

How mindfulness may help people flourish:

Reducing stress and anxiety is one of the main ways that mindfulness may assist people in achieving success. An individual's total well-being, including their physical and mental health, can be significantly impacted by stress and worry. Through increased awareness of their thoughts and emotions and the ability to respond to them in a more constructive and positive way, people can lower their stress levels by practicing mindfulness meditation.

Mindfulness can help people feel more emotionally intelligent in addition to lowering their stress levels. The ability to identify and control one's own emotions as well as comprehend and empathize with those of others is a necessary component of emotional intelligence. By engaging in mindfulness exercises, people can increase their self-awareness and improve their capacity for effective emotion regulation. This can help strengthen bonds between people, broaden empathy, and promote general wellbeing.

By sharpening attention and concentration, mindfulness may also promote prosperity. Training the mind to focus on the here and now via mindfulness meditation can enhance attention and productivity in other aspects of life. As a result, people are better able to concentrate on their objectives and succeed in achieving them, which can increase achievement in both personal and professional undertakings.

<u>The benefit of meditation for obtaining wealth:</u>

Another effective strategy for assisting people in achieving riches is meditation. Similar to mindfulness, meditation helps lessen stress and anxiety levels, which can improve one's general well-being. But meditation also has additional advantages that might boost affluence.

The ability to increase one's awareness of oneself is one of the main advantages of meditation. People who meditate can become more conscious of their thoughts, feelings, and physical sensations, which can improve their understanding of themselves and their needs. Greater self-acceptance and self-love can result from this, which can increase overall happiness and contentment.

Meditation can aid people in becoming more self-aware and adopting a more upbeat view of life. Greater pleasure and fulfillment can result from cultivating a sense of gratitude and appreciation for the present moment through meditation. Individuals who do this may find it easier to concentrate on the positive elements of their lives as opposed to ruminating on unpleasant memories or events.

Additionally, meditation can help people access their creativity and intuition, as well as their inner selves. Deeper levels of consciousness and awareness can be accessed by calming the mind and concentrating on the here and now. They may be able to generate fresh perspectives, ideas, and insights as a result, which may help them succeed both personally and professionally.

Finally, mindfulness and meditation are potent skills that may aid people in achieving success in a number of ways. Mindfulness and meditation can assist people in leading more satisfying lives by lowering levels of stress and anxiety, enhancing emotional intelligence, boosting attention and concentration, raising levels of self-awareness, cultivating a more optimistic attitude toward life, and developing their creativity and intuition. The advantages of these procedures outweigh the potential time and effort requirements.

The Power of Positive Affirmations in Achieving Prosperity

A growing number of people utilize positive affirmations to enhance their mental health and foster personal development. Positive affirmations are fundamentally brief, uplifting remarks that are frequently repeated to support a certain notion or viewpoint. Affirmations may be utilized for a variety of goals, such as boosting self-worth, easing anxiety, and even fostering financial success.

Many times, a state of financial plenty and wellbeing is referred to as prosperity. Many individuals think that achieving financial security is something that is beyond their control and that other elements like chance, the state of the economy, or their social standing dictate their financial situation. However, proponents of positive affirmations contend that by using positive affirmations, prosperity may not only be attained but also actively fostered.

Affirmations that are positive affect our thoughts about ourselves and our surroundings. Positive affirmations train our subconscious brains to concentrate on the good things in our lives rather than the bad or our limits when we repeat them frequently. We are better equipped to detect and take advantage of possibilities that may lead to financial wealth if we concentrate on having positive attitudes and beliefs.

"I am abundant" is one of the most often used affirmations to encourage success. The purpose of this statement is to develop an attitude of plenty rather than lack. We are more likely to perceive chances for personal progress and success when we have an abundance mindset. In addition, we are less likely to let fear or self-doubt prevent us from taking risks and making investments that might result in financial gains.

"I am worthy of wealth and success" is another well-known affirmation used to encourage prosperity. This affirmation is intended to counteract unfavorable thoughts and self-talk that can prevent us from reaching financial success. We are more inclined to take action to reach these objectives, such as going for further education, launching a business, or looking for new employment prospects, when we feel that we are deserving of riches and success.

Affirmations can be used to encourage fiscal restraint and wise spending practices. For instance, repeating affirmations like "I spend money wisely" or "I am in control of my finances" might help us stay focused on our monetary objectives and make better financial decisions.

It's crucial to remember that using only positive affirmations won't bring about financial success. Affirmations can assist in shifting our attention and attitude, but in order to provide significant benefits, action must also be taken. For instance, if we want to be financially prosperous, we must also take actionable steps like making a budget, investing in our education or careers, and looking for chances for professional and personal advancement.

Positive affirmations may have a variety of additional advantages for our mental and emotional health, in addition to encouraging financial prosperity. Affirmations, for instance, can boost confidence and self-esteem, ease tension and anxiety, and encourage a sense of inner quiet and harmony. Affirmations help us develop a good mentality so that we may feel more content and satisfied in both our personal and professional endeavors.

It is impossible to exaggerate the effectiveness of positive affirmations in obtaining success. We may improve our chances of obtaining financial prosperity and success by establishing a mindset of abundance, worthiness, and financial discipline. Positive affirmations are simply one weapon in our toolbox for obtaining financial prosperity, and in order to provide genuine results, they must be combined with action and practical initiatives. Anyone may attain financial wealth and lead a meaningful and rich life with commitment, work, and the power of positive affirmations.

Chapter 9

Stay Focused

How to Deal with Distractions and Stay Focused on Your Prosperity Goals

There are diversions everywhere in the modern world. It's getting harder and harder to keep focused on our objectives with the continual assault of notifications on our phones and the never-ending flow of emails in our inbox. When it comes to accomplishing wealth objectives, which frequently demand a high degree of focus and attention, this may be particularly difficult. There are strategies to cope with distractions, though, so you can continue working toward your financial objectives.

<u>Establish priorities and define goals.</u>

Setting definite objectives and priorities is the first step in maintaining focus on your prosperity objectives. This entails carefully outlining your goals and ranking them in order of significance after taking the time to define them. It is much simpler to stay focused and avoid distractions when you are aware of your priorities and goals.

<u>Make a strategy for action.</u>

Making an action plan is the next step after deciding on your objectives and goals. This entails segmenting your objectives into more achievable, smaller activities and adding them to your schedule. You'll be able to concentrate on your objectives and fend off distractions by making an action plan.

<u>Remove any unneeded distractions.</u>

Eliminating pointless distractions is one of the best strategies to keep focused on your prosperity objectives. This includes disabling your phone's alerts, shutting down your email client, and eliminating any other distractions that can cause you to lose focus on your objectives. You'll be able to concentrate on the job at hand and make greater progress toward your objectives if you remove distractions.

<u>Frequently pause.</u>

Taking regular pauses might really help you stay focused on your prosperity objectives, despite the fact that it may seem paradoxical. This is due to the fact that breaks give your brain a chance to relax and regenerate, which might aid in your ability to focus and remain attentive when you return to your task. Therefore, be sure to take frequent breaks during the day and utilize that time to refresh your energy and refocus your attention.

<u>Practice being aware.</u>

Maintaining focus on your objectives for financial prosperity requires the application of mindfulness. This entails living in the present and giving your all to the work at hand. When you engage in mindfulness practice, you'll be able to keep your attention on your goals and ward off distractions.

Use uplifting statements.

A helpful method for maintaining focus on your financial objectives is the use of positive affirmations. This entails making use of encouraging words to bolster your self-confidence and belief in your capacity to succeed. You can maintain your motivation and attention despite obstacles and distractions by employing positive affirmations.

Be in the company of encouraging individuals.

Finally, it's crucial to surround yourself with positive individuals who can encourage your continued commitment to your financial aspirations. This entails surrounding oneself with others who have faith in your potential to succeed. Maintaining your motivation and attention to work toward your objectives is considerably simpler when you have a network of encouraging individuals around.

In conclusion, overcoming distractions and maintaining your attention on your financial objectives might be difficult, but they are attainable. You may maintain concentration and reach your prosperity objectives by establishing clear goals and priorities, developing a plan of action, removing needless distractions, taking frequent pauses, practicing mindfulness, utilizing positive affirmations, and surrounding yourself with encouraging people. Keep in mind that success is a journey rather than a destination and that the secret to reaching your objectives and leading the life of your dreams is to remain focused.

The Importance of Taking Care of Your Physical and Mental Health for Achieving Prosperity

Being prosperous involves more than just being financially secure or professionally successful. It also entails living a balanced, healthy lifestyle on both a physical and mental level. In order to flourish, you must take care of your physical and mental health since it has an impact on all facets of your life, including your personal relationships, work, and general well-being.

Physical well-being and success:

Being physically well allows you to go about your everyday business and achieve your goals, which is the basis of wealth. In order to stay physically fit, one must follow a balanced diet, engage in regular exercise, and get enough sleep. These routines aid in maintaining physical fitness, which boosts vigor, enhances cognitive ability, and boosts overall productivity.

For the purpose of preserving physical health, a nutritious diet is crucial. It gives your body the nutrition it requires for healthy functioning and illness prevention. For optimum health, a diet high in fruits, vegetables, whole grains, and lean proteins is advised. Maintaining a healthy weight is also facilitated by eating a balanced diet, which is crucial for avoiding chronic diseases like diabetes and heart disease.

Physical health also depends on regular exercise. Muscle, bone, and joint health are all improved by exercise. Additionally, it lowers the chance of developing chronic illnesses, including diabetes, obesity, and cardiovascular disease. Additionally, exercise helps with sleep, which is crucial for both physical and mental wellness.

Physical health also benefits greatly from getting enough sleep. To improve physical performance and general wellbeing, your body needs enough sleep to repair and regenerate. Numerous health difficulties, including an elevated risk of obesity, heart disease, and mental health problems like anxiety and depression, can be brought on by sleep deprivation.

Mental wellness and success:

In terms of obtaining affluence, mental health is as crucial as physical health. Your emotional, psychological, and social well-being are all included in your mental health. It has an impact on your day-to-day thoughts, emotions, and behaviors. For general well-being and enjoyment, maintaining excellent mental health is crucial.

Several behaviors contribute to good mental health, including stress management, mindfulness exercises, and asking for assistance when necessary. Good mental health requires effective stress management. A variety of health issues, including anxiety, depression, and cardiovascular disease, can be brought on by high levels of stress. Deep breathing, yoga, and other stress-reduction practices can help lower stress levels and enhance mental health.

Additionally, mindfulness is necessary for excellent mental wellness. Being mindful requires accepting things as they are in the present moment. It can aid in lowering tension, elevating mood, and enhancing general wellbeing. Deep breathing exercises, yoga, and meditation are all mindfulness techniques.

For healthy mental health, it's also crucial to ask for assistance when you need it. It may be difficult to handle mental health issues alone, so getting support from a mental health expert can be very beneficial. In addressing mental health conditions including anxiety, sadness, and trauma, mental health experts may offer support and direction.

<u>How physical and mental health are related:</u>

Maintaining good physical and mental health might help each other since they are interdependent. For instance, regular exercise has been demonstrated to enhance mental health by lowering the signs of despair and anxiety. Additionally, exercise encourages improved sleep, which is necessary for mental wellness.

The same is true for sustaining healthy mental and physical health. Heart disease, diabetes, and chronic pain are just a few of the physical health issues that stress, worry, and depression may cause. Controlling these mental health conditions can enhance overall wellbeing and physical health.

Prosperity can be attained through a balanced lifestyle.
It's crucial to look after your physical and mental health if you want to flourish. You may attain your objectives and have a full life by adopting a balanced lifestyle that includes a nutritious diet, regular exercise, enough sleep, and excellent mental health practices.

Living a balanced lifestyle may bring you success in a number of ways. It can increase your output and performance at work, as you'll have greater vigor and concentration to finish jobs quickly. Maintaining a healthy lifestyle will also help your interpersonal connections since it will make it easier for you to cope with stress and keep a positive attitude toward life. You may improve your connections with others by practicing good mental health habits like mindfulness and getting assistance when you need it.

A balanced lifestyle can also increase your financial well-being in addition to these advantages. You may lower your chance of developing chronic health issues that can be expensive to treat by maintaining strong physical and mental health. Additionally, you could discover that you have more vigor and concentration to pursue your work objectives, which might result in financial success.

In general, maintaining good physical and mental health is necessary for prospering in all spheres of life. Prioritizing self-care activities, including a nutritious diet, consistent exercise, getting enough sleep, and maintaining excellent mental health, is crucial. You can increase your general well-being and have a satisfying life by taking good care of your body and mind.

The Role of Creativity and Innovation in Finding New Ways to Achieve Prosperity

Even though the terms creativity and innovation are frequently used interchangeably, they each have distinct definitions. Innovation is the capacity to turn novel ideas into workable solutions, whereas creativity is the capacity to produce new ideas. Innovating and being creative are both essential components of discovering new paths to riches. We'll go through how innovation and creativity may boost the economy, raise standards of living, and open up new commercial and personal prospects below.

Innovation and Creativity as Economic Growth Drivers:

Since they assist organizations and individuals in coming up with fresh approaches to issues, developing new goods, and boosting productivity, creativity and innovation are crucial forces behind economic progress. For instance, the growth of the internet has fundamentally changed how people interact, collaborate, and conduct business. The invention of the internet was made possible by the imagination and ingenuity of people and organizations that were able to think outside the box and develop fresh strategies for bridging geographical distances.

The emergence of new industries is significantly aided by creativity and innovation. For instance, the development of the renewable energy sector has been fueled by the imagination and ingenuity of people and organizations that recognized a chance to develop more ecologically friendly and sustainable forms of energy. This has not only reduced carbon emissions but also given rise to new job prospects and economic chances.

<u>Better living conditions:</u>

It is impossible to exaggerate the contribution of creativity and invention to raising living standards. For instance, better health outcomes for individuals all around the world have been brought about through the development of new medical technology and therapies. Automation and robotics have also enhanced manufacturing productivity and efficiency, which has reduced consumer costs and broadened access to goods and services.

Additionally, innovation and creativity can result in the development of brand- new goods and services that improve people's lives. For instance, the advent of smartphones has completely changed how individuals interact with one another, do business, and get information. Additionally, it has given companies new chances to connect with clients and offer services in creative ways.

<u>Making New Possibilities:</u>

For both corporations and individuals, creativity and innovation may open up new possibilities. For instance, the creation of novel products and technologies has the potential to expand markets and generate new sources of income. Additionally, by using their imagination, firms might find untapped markets or growth opportunities.

Additionally, innovation and inventiveness may upend established marketplaces and pose a threat to dominant businesses. Increased competition and innovation may result from this, which may lower prices and raise the caliber of goods and services.

Individuals can benefit from new opportunities brought about by innovation and creativity. For instance, the growth of the gig economy has given people new chances to work on their own terms and follow their hobbies. Additionally, people are now better able to commercialize their talents and experiences because of the expansion of internet platforms.

Challenges to Innovation and Creativity:

Even though creativity and invention have numerous advantages, they can also face obstacles that prevent them from growing. The resistance of people and organizations to change is one of the main obstacles. Many people are averse to change and could consider novel concepts or methods to be dangerous.

In addition, obstacles to innovation and creativity are frequently financial and legal. For instance, it may be expensive to create new technologies or goods, and it may be challenging to introduce new items to the market due to regulatory constraints.

Economic progress, higher living standards, and the emergence of new possibilities all depend on creativity and innovation. They may result in the growth of new businesses, the production of more employment, and an improvement in people's quality of life. Creativity and invention must, however, also overcome some obstacles. Individuals and companies must accept change, and governments must promote creativity and innovation if they want to see success. By doing this, we can improve the future for both present and future generations.

The Power of Leveraging Technology and Automation for Achieving Prosperity

Technology and automation are becoming effective instruments for creating success in today's environment. Businesses and individuals may use automation to simplify their operations, improve productivity, and ultimately grow their bottom line thanks to the quick improvements in technology. Automation's and technology's influence cannot be understated since they have the ability to revolutionize whole sectors and alter how we live and work.

Increasing productivity is one of the key advantages of using automation and technology. Businesses can now complete jobs more quickly and precisely than ever before because of automation solutions like software, robots, and machine learning algorithms. Automation has been utilized, for instance, in the manufacturing industry to speed up production and cut down on the time needed to make items. Larger output levels and greater corporate profitability are the results of this.

Technology and automation have the ability to save costs while simultaneously boosting production. Businesses may reduce labor expenses and save time by automating repetitive jobs and simplifying procedures. For instance, a business can eliminate the requirement for customer care agents by using an automated customer support system, which lowers labor expenses. Automation may also lower mistakes and enhance quality control, which can result in fewer product flaws and lower expenses for product recalls and returns.

Expanding into new markets is another advantage of utilizing automation and technology. Social media and the internet have made it possible for companies to connect with clients globally. Businesses now have more chances to grow their clientele and boost profits thanks to this. Additionally, automation has enabled companies to provide clients with tailored goods and services, which can boost client happiness and loyalty.

Technology and automation have had a big impact on the work economy as well. The automation of certain occupations may result in the creation of new ones in industries like data analysis, programming, and robotics. There is now a greater need for people with specific talents in these fields as a result of the growth of automation.

People may set themselves up for success in these expanding industries by investing in education and training programs.

Technology and automation not only bring advantages for people and businesses, but they also have the ability to solve some of the most urgent problems in the world. Automation may be utilized, for instance, to enhance food distribution and production, which can help solve concerns with hunger and malnutrition. Automation may also be utilized to increase access to crucial services like healthcare, education, and others.

It's crucial to remember that technology and automation should only be used properly. It is crucial to think about the ethical implications of automation as technology develops and to make sure that it is applied in a way that benefits society as a whole. Making sure that people and organizations have access to the tools and training they need to thrive in a world that is becoming more and more automated is also crucial.

In conclusion, it is impossible to overlook how automation and technology may lead to wealth. The advantages of automation are obvious, ranging from boosting production and cutting costs to entering new markets and tackling global concerns. To guarantee that automation is employed in a way that benefits society as a whole, it is crucial to approach it cautiously. Businesses and people may position themselves for success in a world that is becoming increasingly automated by using technology and automation wisely.

How to Overcome Procrastination and Stay Productive Towards your Prosperity Goals

People frequently battle with procrastination. It is the practice of procrastinating or putting off chores or actions, frequently to the point that one feels stressed out and overwhelmed. Procrastination is an issue since it may reduce your productivity and keep you from accomplishing your financial objectives. However, there are a number of methods you may employ to avoid procrastinating and continue working toward your objectives.

<u>Determine the underlying reason for procrastination.</u>

Procrastination may be brought on by a number of things, including overload, a lack of desire, and a fear of failure. Finding the source of your procrastination is crucial if you want to conquer it. Spend some time thinking about why you are delaying, then put your ideas on paper. You may use this to clarify your problem and create a strategy for dealing with it.

<u>Divide your objectives into more achievable, smaller activities.</u>

The overwhelming immensity of one's ambitions is one of the key causes of procrastination. Divide your objectives into more doable, smaller chores to prevent this. You'll find it simpler to begin and maintain your attention on your goals as a result. If your objective is to create a book, for instance, divide it into smaller tasks like organizing the chapters, doing research, and writing the preface.

Establish a schedule.

A timetable will help you stay organized and on task. Establish a schedule for the day or the week and set out precise hours for each task. By doing so, you may organize your duties according to priority and make sure that you are moving closer to your objectives. To prevent burnout, be sure to plan breaks.

Don't get distracted.

One of the biggest barriers to productivity is distraction. Identify the distractions in your environment, such as social media, television, or email, and get rid of them. To help you stay focused, you may also employ tools like page blockers or time-tracking applications.

Implement the Pomodoro Technique.

A time-management technique called the Pomodoro Technique involves working for a certain amount of time, usually 25 minutes, and then taking a little rest. By dividing the workload into digestible halves, this technique aids in concentration and productivity. Take a longer pause of about 20 to 30 minutes following four Pomodoro sessions.

Identify a partner for accountability.

Someone holding you responsible might serve as strong motivation. A friend or mentor who can check in on your progress and provide support and encouragement makes a good accountability partner. This might support your efforts to stay motivated and on track.

Celebrate little victories.

Celebrating modest victories is crucial for maintaining motivation and productivity. Spend some time celebrating your accomplishments and rewarding yourself for your efforts. This can help you stay inspired and motivated while you work toward your objectives.

Exercise self-care.

Forging ahead with productivity and overcoming procrastination requires self- care. Make time for self-care pursuits, including physical activity, meditation, and family time. You'll feel refreshed and motivated to keep working toward your objectives.

Stay upbeat.

To beat procrastination and accomplish your goals, you must have an optimistic outlook. Instead of wallowing in your disappointments, concentrate on the progress you have achieved. Keep in mind that setbacks are a normal part of the process and that each one is a chance for development and learning.

Assistance should be sought.

It may be a good idea to seek professional assistance if you discover that you are still having trouble with procrastination despite attempting these tactics. You can create a strategy to conquer your procrastination with the assistance of a therapist or coach.

It's crucial to keep in mind that overcoming procrastination is a process, and it could take some time and work to see real results. However, by constantly putting these ideas into practice, you may create wholesome routines that will support your continued productivity, motivation, and concentration on your wealth objectives.

It might also be beneficial to think about why you value reaching your prosperity objectives. Knowing your unique driving force and life vision may keep you motivated and committed to your objectives, even in the face of adversity.

Finally, it's critical to cultivate self-compassion and kindness toward oneself. Keep in mind that everyone experiences procrastination issues occasionally and that failures are a normal part of the process. Be kind to yourself and keep working toward your objectives.

In conclusion, overcoming procrastination and continuing to work towards your prosperity goals entails figuring out the reasons behind your procrastination, breaking down your goals into manageable tasks, scheduling your work, eliminating distractions, using the Pomodoro Technique, finding an accountability partner, celebrating small victories, engaging in self-care, remaining upbeat, and getting help if necessary. You may beat procrastination and reach your wealth objectives by employing these techniques regularly and concentrating on your own unique drive and life vision.

Chapter 10
Enjoy the Journey

The Importance of Being Flexible and Adaptable in Achieving Prosperity

Being adaptive and flexible is perhaps more crucial than ever in the environment we live in today. Whether it be in one's personal, professional, or social contexts, prosperity depends on one's capacity to adjust to changing events and circumstances.

First of all, being adaptive and flexible enables us to take advantage of newly presented opportunities. Opportunities frequently present themselves unexpectedly in today's competitive environment and call for swift responses. Those who are dogmatic and inflexible in their thinking may overlook these possibilities or find it difficult to seize them. Conversely, people who are adaptive may readily change their plans and methods to take advantage of these chances, which can improve prosperity.

Take a small company owner who has a physical store as an illustration. The owner may have trouble surviving if they are rigid and reluctant to change with shifting customer preferences. However, if the business owner is flexible and eager to adopt new technologies and online sales channels, they could be able to grow their clientele and boost their income, which would result in higher affluence.

Second, flexibility and adaptability help us get through difficulties and barriers. No matter how diligently we prepare, there will inevitably be unforeseen difficulties and barriers. When faced with these difficulties, people who are rigid and inflexible in thought may get paralyzed or stuck, whereas those who are adaptable may easily change their ideas and come up with novel ways to get past the difficulties.

Think of a student, for instance, who has trouble with a certain academic subject. The student may continue to struggle and maybe fail the class if they are rigid and reluctant to change their study habits. The student may be able to overcome the challenge and succeed if they are adaptive and ready to attempt different study methods, ask for assistance from a tutor, or work with classmates. This success will increase their chances of success in both their academic and future professional endeavors.

Thirdly, flexibility and adaptability help us remain current and competitive in the industries we choose. Industries and technology are continually changing in today's quick-paced world, and those who are rigid and unable to change risk being swiftly outmoded or irrelevant. The ability to adapt to these changes and stay on top of the game, however, can result in more riches and success for individuals who possess this ability.

Take a software developer, for instance, who focuses on a specific programming language. The developer may have trouble finding employment or be passed over for advancement if they are rigid and hesitant to learn new languages or technologies. The developer may be able to remain relevant and competitive in the job market, which may boost prosperity and success, if they are versatile and eager to acquire new skills and technologies.

Being adaptive and flexible can enhance our general wellbeing in addition to these particular advantages. Being adaptive helps us deal with stress, uncertainty, and change better, which can increase our resilience and mental health. Being flexible also enables us to explore a variety of chances and experiences, which may result in a life that is richer and more meaningful.

In conclusion, success in today's world of fast change depends on one's ability to be adaptive and flexible. Those who are adaptable may readily take advantage of new possibilities, get beyond barriers and problems, stay relevant and competitive, and attain total wellbeing and contentment in any situation, whether it be in a personal, professional, or social environment. In order to reach greater prosperity and success, it is crucial to build a mindset of adaptation and flexibility in all facets of our lives.

The Role of Gratitude and Generosity in Achieving Prosperity

Two important ideas that are essential to reaching prosperity are gratitude and generosity. Although these ideas can appear unconnected at first glance, they are actually much interconnected. The emotion of gratitude is one of appreciation and thanksgiving for the possibilities and gifts in one's life. The act of giving to others, whether via deeds of kindness, monetary contributions, or other methods, is known as generosity. Below, we'll look at how generosity and appreciation are related to success and how they do so.

Although material wealth and financial success are frequently linked to prosperity, prosperity is much more than that. True abundance embraces all facets of life, such as good health, fulfilling relationships, and personal contentment. Positivity, a strong work ethic, and a willingness to take initiative are necessary for prosperity. This mentality must include both gratitude and generosity because they foster a sense of plenty and optimism that may help people succeed more in all facets of life.

Prosperity is built on a foundation of gratitude. We draw more of the same into our lives when we are thankful for what we already have. This is because feeling grateful is a strong, good emotion that tells the universe that we are grateful for the benefits in our lives. By concentrating on what we have to be thankful for, we invite in additional possibilities and benefits, which may result in increased prosperity.

Gratitude not only brings greater prosperity into our lives, but it also fosters a more upbeat mindset. Negative emotions like stress, worry, and despair are less likely to drag us down when we concentrate on the positive aspects of our lives. As a result, we are better able to concentrate our efforts on attaining our goals, which may then result in greater success in both our personal and professional lives.

Another essential element for reaching riches is generosity. Giving to others, whether it be via deeds of kindness or monetary contributions, has a good knock- on effect that may be advantageous to both of us. Since we are sharing our gifts with others and fostering a happier environment, generosity promotes richness and flow in our lives.

Being generous fosters a feeling of wealth and strengthens bonds between people. Giving to others fosters a relationship based on mutual respect and trust that may help us succeed both personally and professionally. We may start a beneficial cycle of giving and getting by assisting others in realizing their aspirations, which can result in increased success for all parties.

A mentality of wealth and happiness is a key component of both gratitude and generosity. We are more inclined to be kind with our time, money, and energy when we are thankful for what we have. Similar to how giving to others fosters feelings of gratitude and appreciation, doing so might increase our own success.

Focusing on the here and now is one of the keys to developing appreciation and giving. We are more likely to see the benefits in our lives and give of our time and money when we are completely present in the moment. This may be accomplished by engaging in activities that foster a sense of presentences and awareness, such as meditation, mindfulness, and gratitude writing.

The ability to put others' needs first is another essential skill for developing appreciation and generosity. We are more inclined to be kind and contribute when we are considering the needs of others, since we are driven by a desire to support them. This may be accomplished through helping others, giving to a good cause, or just being there for someone who needs a sympathetic ear.

The Power of Goal-Setting and Action-Planning for Achieving Prosperity

Two essential components for obtaining success are goal-setting and action planning. It might be difficult to prioritize our energy, time, and resources if we don't create specific, realistic goals. Similar to how it might be challenging to make our ambitions a reality without a clear action plan. This chapter will examine the importance of defining goals and creating action plans, as well as how they might aid in our pursuit of success.

First and foremost, goal-setting is the act of figuring out what we want to achieve, the measures necessary to do so, and the deadline for doing so. Setting goals has a lot of power since it may give you drive and direction. We lay out a plan for success when we have a clear and explicit goal. We are aware of our destination and the steps required to get there. Goal-setting also gives us a sense of direction and drive. When we are focused and work hard toward a goal, we are more likely to persevere through difficulties.

Setting goals may aid in directing and motivating us as well as in the organization of our efforts. We all have a limited amount of time and money, so choosing where to put our attention may be difficult. We may prioritize our efforts and devote more time and resources to the tasks that will enable us to accomplish our goals, though, when we have set clear goals. For instance, if we want to raise our income, we might concentrate on learning new skills or looking for new career options.

But simply defining objectives won't help us attain them; we also need to have a clear action plan. The measures we must take to accomplish our goals are outlined in an action plan, along with the dates, checkpoints, and materials we will need. Action planning's strength rests in its capacity to divide our objectives into doable stages, making them more reachable and less intimidating.

Action planning also helps us maintain our attention and organization. We can keep on track and make sure that we are moving closer to our goals by dividing them into smaller tasks and giving each task a deadline. Action planning can also assist us in identifying probable problems or difficulties and creating backup plans to deal with them.

Setting goals and creating an action plan may help us take charge of our lives, which is one of their main advantages. By establishing specific objectives and developing a detailed action plan, we take charge of our destiny. We are causing things to occur rather than waiting for them to. This feeling of control can inspire us to act and advance toward our objectives by empowering and encouraging us.

Setting goals and creating an action plan also enable us to track our progress. We can monitor our progress and make necessary modifications when we establish clear goals and develop a well-defined action plan. We can see how far we've come and how much closer we are to attaining our goals, which keeps us motivated and focused.

Goal-setting and action planning can also assist us in acquiring critical abilities and traits that are necessary for obtaining wealth. For instance, establishing objectives necessitates being proactive, imaginative, and strategic. We also need to be tenacious and tough, since there may be setbacks and challenges along the way. Similar to organization, discipline, and accountability, action planning calls for these qualities in us. These abilities and traits are important for both personal and professional development as well as obtaining success.

To sum up, the strength of goal-setting and action planning resides in their capacity to offer motivation, focus, and direction. We can take charge of our future, prioritize our efforts, and track our progress by defining clear, precise goals and developing a well-defined action plan. Additionally, these procedures can assist us in acquiring critical abilities and traits that are necessary for obtaining prosperity.

How to Create a Supportive Team for Achieving Prosperity

For every firm to be successful, building a supportive team is crucial. A group that collaborates well and encourages one another may achieve amazing things. It's critical to establish an atmosphere in which each team member is recognized and cherished. We'll go through the actions you can take to assemble a cohesive team that can help you succeed.

<u>Specify expectations and goals in detail.</u>

Setting clear objectives and expectations is the first step in building a cooperative team. The group must be aware of the goals they are aiming to achieve as well as their duties. Outlining clear goals, dates, and milestones can help you achieve this. It's easier to prevent misunderstandings when everyone is on the same page. To make sure that the team is aware of the expectations placed on them, it is crucial to properly communicate those objectives and expectations to them.

Encourage open dialogue.

The foundation for creating a cohesive team is effective communication. Members of the team should be encouraged to express their thoughts and opinions. In meetings, make sure that everyone has an opportunity to speak and that their opinions are heard. Openness, honesty, and respect should characterize communication. A cohesive team is one that listens to one another and communicates well.

Promoting a happy workplace.

Building a supportive team requires creating a pleasant work atmosphere. Promote an environment of respect, trust, and responsibility. Celebrate successes and acknowledge team members' efforts. Encouraging group cooperation requires creating a pleasant work atmosphere. Promote an environment of respect, trust, and responsibility. A supportive team may be fostered, and a sense of belonging can be increased in a favorable work environment.

Offer chances for development and training.

A fantastic way to demonstrate your support for your staff is to invest in training and development opportunities for them. It promotes the team members' professional growth as well as the organization as a whole. Give people the chance to get coaching, mentorship, and training. Encourage team members to go to seminars and conferences. This investment in your team contributes to the formation of a cohesive group that is dedicated to attaining success.

<u>Encourage creativity and innovation.</u>

Prosperity can only be attained through innovation and ingenuity. Encourage the members of your team to think creatively and independently. Support innovation by giving new ventures resources and finance. Encourage taking chances and trying new things. Celebrate mistakes as chances for development and learning. You can create a supportive team that is eager to take chances and push limits by fostering innovation and creativity.

<u>Encourage a culture of ongoing development.</u>

A team that is dedicated to constant development is supportive. Encourage your team members to strive for greatness and learn from their failures. Establish a culture that values development and learning. Encourage your team members to ask for feedback and apply it to their work. You may create a group of individuals who are dedicated to reaching success by developing a culture of continual development.

<u>Set a good example.</u>

Finally, it's crucial for a leader to set an example. By being supportive yourself, you may model support for your team. Be honest and transparent when communicating. Encourage a good workplace atmosphere. By providing training and development opportunities, you can invest in your workforce. Encourage creativity and innovation. Encourage a culture of ongoing development. By setting a positive example, you inspire a cooperative group of people who are dedicated to creating wealth.

In conclusion, building a strong team is crucial to the success of any firm. Setting clear objectives and goals, promoting open communication, building a healthy work environment, offering chances for training and development, stimulating innovation and creativity, developing a culture of continuous improvement, and setting an example are all necessary. You may create a team that is dedicated to reaching prosperity by following these procedures.

The Importance of Enjoying the Journey Towards Achieving Prosperity

Being successful and thriving, both financially and in one's personal life, is the condition of prosperity. It makes sense that many individuals aspire to this objective. But the path to riches is just as important—if not more important— than the destination itself. We discover new things, develop, and finally transform into the kind of people who can succeed along the way. In this chapter, we will discuss the significance of taking pleasure in the path to riches.

The procedure is more sustainable in the first place when you are having fun along the way. The pursuit of prosperity is not something that can be done quickly. It calls for prolonged periods of hard effort, devotion, and perseverance. If we approach the path to riches as a means to an end, we risk becoming demoralized and exhausted along the way. But if we can learn to appreciate the process, we can persevere with our efforts for a longer time. We are more likely to remain motivated and dedicated to the work at hand when we appreciate what we are doing.

Second, taking pleasure in the path gives a sense of accomplishment and satisfaction. While obtaining affluence as a final objective is vital, the process of getting there is what gives our lives meaning and purpose. We develop as people when we participate in challenging activities that force us outside of our comfort zones. A sense of contentment and happiness that cannot be attained by only achieving a financial objective can be attained through this progress. We create connections, learn new skills, and go through personal development throughout the voyage.

Third, taking pleasure in the trip enables us to fully appreciate the present. We risk missing out on the present if we just focus on achieving success in the long run. We risk losing sight of the tiny successes along the way because we are so focused on obtaining our objective. We may become more attentive to our experiences and more present by learning to appreciate the trip. Instead of concentrating just on the outcome, we may enjoy the beauty of the process.

Fourth, having fun on the trip encourages resilience. Achieving prosperity will include overcoming challenges and failures. We could get disheartened and give up if we see these setbacks as failures. But if we can learn to love the ride, we may see these failures as chances to improve.

By strengthening our resilience, we are better able to deal with the difficulties that life throws at us. Instead of allowing challenges to defeat us, we learn to adapt and conquer them.

Fifth, having fun along the way encourages a development mentality. A growth mindset is the conviction that we can improve our skills with effort and commitment. We are more likely to adopt a growth mentality when we enjoy the path to success. Instead of seeing difficulties as obstacles to our achievement, we see them as chances to grow and learn. This style of thinking enables us to approach our objectives with confidence and optimism, knowing that we can get through any challenges that may arise.

In conclusion, the process of reaching affluence is just as crucial as the ultimate result, if not more so. We may increase the sustainability of the process, discover pleasure and happiness, appreciate the present moment, build resilience, and adopt a growth mindset by learning to enjoy the trip. In the end, it is through the journey that we develop as individuals and become capable of obtaining success.

Chapter 11
Gratitude & Appreciation

The Power of Gratitude and Appreciation for Prosperity: *Cultivating Abundance*

We may generate richness and success in our lives by being grateful and appreciative. We attract more of the same things into our lives when we are thankful for what we have and appreciate the people and possibilities around us. The power of appreciation and gratitude, as well as how to nurture them to attract plenty, will be discussed here.

Let's start by defining what we mean by prosperity and plenty. The state of plenty refers to having more than enough of what we need or want. It's a sensation of being content with what we have and a sense of completeness. A state of financial success and well-being is called prosperity. It is the capacity to enjoy life's comforts in addition to being able to fulfill our basic requirements.

Recognizing and expressing gratitude for the positive aspects of our lives is the practice of gratitude. We change our perspective from one of scarcity to one of plenty when we concentrate on what we have rather than what we lack. Even in challenging circumstances, we begin to notice the chances and benefits all around us. We feel happier, more pleased, and less stressed when we are grateful.

Recognizing and valuing the people, objects, and events in our lives is the discipline of appreciation. We recognize something's value and significance when we enjoy it. We thank it for being a part of our lives. We can foster healthy connections and see the beauty in the world around us by showing appreciation for it.

So how can we develop a spirit of gratitude and respect for wealth? Here are a few tips:

Keep an appreciation diary.

We can focus on the good and develop an abundant attitude by keeping a daily gratitude journal. List three things for which you are thankful every day. They may be substantial or intangible, large or small. We begin to attract more of the same by frequently reminding ourselves of the positive things in our lives.

Engage in mindfulness.

Being in the present without passing judgment is the practice of mindfulness. Being attentive makes us more conscious of our thoughts and emotions. We can see them without being enmeshed in them. This encourages us to build a spirit of thankfulness and appreciation for the here and now, despite its imperfections.

Show them your gratitude.

When we show others our appreciation, we not only make them feel good, but we also build wholesome connections. Spend some time expressing your thanks to someone for their assistance or being in your life. This can be done through a straightforward thank-you message, a compliment, or an emotional chat.

Give back.

Fostering an attitude of appreciation and plenty may be achieved through helping others. We feel good about ourselves and our capacity to have a positive effect when we help others. This might be as easy as giving your time to a local charity or making a donation to a cause you believe in.

Practice affirmations.

By repeating encouraging words to oneself, affirmations help to reinforce a happy outlook. For instance, "I appreciate the people and experiences that bring joy to my life" or "I am grateful for the abundance in my life." These affirmations can help us develop an abundance mindset and attract more wealth into our lives if we repeat them frequently.

Finally, practicing appreciation and thankfulness is a potent method to attract riches and prosperity into our lives. We attract more of the same by thinking positively and showing gratitude for what we already have. We create satisfying connections and a sense of purpose by giving value to the people and situations in our lives. Try adopting these routines into your life to observe how they might alter your perspective and increase your abundance.

Building a Prosperous Business: Entrepreneurship and Leadership Skills

Building a successful firm requires both entrepreneurial spirit and strong leadership qualities. Any successful business, from start-ups to established businesses, depends on them. The significance of these talents and how to acquire them to build a successful business will be covered.

The process of founding or launching a new business endeavor is called entrepreneurship. To build a successful business, a person must find a business opportunity, design a business strategy, and then put that plan into action. Successful businesspeople have a certain set of abilities that allow them to take chances, spot opportunities, and come up with original solutions to issues.

The capacity to spot possibilities is one of the most essential abilities for entrepreneurship. Entrepreneurs need to be able to spot market opportunities and pinpoint potential clients. Additionally, they must be able to evaluate a company's idea viability and create a strategy to implement it. This necessitates a thorough comprehension of market dynamics, consumer requirements, and industry trends.

Risk-taking is yet another crucial entrepreneurial ability. To develop their company ideas, entrepreneurs must be ready to take calculated risks. Additionally, they must be able to modify their strategy in response to shifting market conditions. High levels of resiliency and a readiness to learn from mistakes are needed for this.

Building a successful firm requires strong leadership abilities. Leaders determine a company's vision and direction, as well as the growth and motivation of its employees. Effective leaders combine technical and soft skills to efficiently manage people, resources, and operations.

Communication is one of the most crucial leadership abilities. Clear and effective communication of a leader's vision, objectives, and expectations is essential. Additionally, they must be able to solicit input, respond to issues, and offer helpful criticism. Transparency and accountability are key components of a culture of effective communication and are essential for developing credibility.

Making decisions is a crucial leadership trait. Leaders need to be able to act promptly and firmly when faced with difficult choices. Additionally, they must be able to weigh the advantages and disadvantages of many possibilities in order to determine the best course of action. A mix of analytical and strategic thinking, as well as the capacity to deal with ambiguity and uncertainty, is necessary for effective decision-making.

Entrepreneurs and executives must continuously hone and grow their abilities in order to construct a successful firm. This necessitates a dedication to ongoing development, self-reflection, and lifelong learning. The following are some techniques for honing these abilities:

- Attend industry conferences, sign up for trade associations, and network with other business owners and executives. Building relationships, exchanging ideas, and learning from others are all made possible via networking.

- Mentoring. Look for mentors with expertise in your sector or business. Mentors may help you learn new skills and give advice, support, and feedback.

- Continue your education by enrolling in classes, attending seminars, and earning certifications to advance your learning. Maintaining your knowledge of industry trends and best practices may also be achieved through continued education.

- Practice. Develop your abilities by accepting new challenges, assuming leadership positions voluntarily, and looking for chances to take the reins and make choices.

In conclusion, developing entrepreneurial and leadership abilities is essential for creating a successful company. Entrepreneurs need to be able to spot possibilities, take calculated risks, and carry out their ideas successfully. Leaders need to be able to communicate clearly, establish a clear vision, and make difficult decisions. Entrepreneurs and leaders must be dedicated to lifetime learning, networking, mentoring, continuous education, and practice in order to acquire these talents. By doing this, they may establish profitable businesses that flourish in the fast-paced and very competitive business world of today.

Creating a Prosperous Career: Finding Purpose and Fulfillment

A successful job involves more than merely earning a big income or moving up the corporate ladder. It's about finding meaning and satisfaction in your career. A feeling of purpose helps you stay motivated and involved in your work, which improves job satisfaction, productivity, and general well-being. Here are some actions you can take to build a successful job that reflects your beliefs and fulfills you.

<u>Decide what you believe in and what you like.</u>

Identify your values and interests to begin. What is important to you? What interests you deeply? What kind of work would you like to do? Consider the activities and interests outside of work that provide you joy and fulfillment. Do you like to create new things, solve issues, or assist others? Make your professional decisions with this information.

<u>Make objectives.</u>

Set precise, measurable, attainable, relevant, and time-bound (SMART) objectives after you've developed an understanding of your beliefs and interests. For instance, if you wish to work in the healthcare sector, your SMART objective may be to earn a nursing degree within the next three years. Setting goals helps you concentrate your efforts and gives you something to strive towards.

Examine your career possibilities.

Look at several job paths that fit with your beliefs and hobbies. To learn more about the daily tasks, required skills, and possible employment advancement, speak to individuals working in those sectors. Participate in employment fairs, networking gatherings, or informative interviews to gain additional knowledge about the sector.

Obtain pertinent experience.

By taking up internships, part-time employment, volunteering, or job shadowing, you may get experience in the sector you want to work in. You will have a deeper comprehension of the sector as a result, and it will also help you create a network of connections. You can also build transferrable abilities that are useful in any line of work.

Perpetual learning.

By reading trade journals, going to conferences, or taking courses, you may keep abreast of market developments and best practices. You will gain new information and abilities as a result, increasing your value to companies.

Network.

Building a successful career requires networking. Participate in professional gatherings, sign up for associations, or establish LinkedIn connections. These contacts may result in career openings, mentorship, or helpful guidance.

Take on challenges.

Embrace difficulties and see them as chances to advance. Even if they are outside of your comfort zone, don't be scared to take on new duties or initiatives. This will assist you in learning new skills and demonstrating your worth to companies.

Be strong.

It takes time and effort to build a successful career. Along the road, you can encounter obstacles or rejection. Being resilient and keeping a good outlook are crucial. Keep pushing forward, keep your eyes on your objectives, and draw lessons from your missteps.

Identify your mission and happiness.

Finding meaning and satisfaction in your job is ultimately the key to developing a successful career. This can be accomplished through assisting people, coming up with a novel idea, resolving a conflict, or supporting a worthwhile cause. You are more likely to be content and successful in your job when you are engaged in work that gives you meaning and fulfillment.

Therefore, more than only technical know-how and work experience are needed to build a successful career. To do this, you must know your beliefs, create objectives, research professional possibilities, accumulate relevant experience, continue learning, network, accept obstacles, be resilient, and find meaning and joy in your job. You may develop a profession that reflects your beliefs, provides you satisfaction, and success by following the steps listed above.

Building a Strong Foundation for Prosperity: Mindset and Attitude

In order to fulfill one's ambitions and goals, one must lay a solid foundation for prosperity. Possessing the proper mindset and attitude is among the foundation's most important elements. Success, happiness, and general well-being are significantly influenced by a person's perspective and attitude.

People who have an optimistic outlook and attitude are better able to handle challenges, deal with adversity, and recover from failures. On the other side, a pessimistic outlook and attitude can prevent people from moving forward by causing self-doubt, dread, and inactivity. To lay a solid foundation for prosperity, it is crucial to create a good mindset and attitude.

Having a growth mindset is one of the first steps in creating a positive outlook and attitude. A growth mindset is the conviction that one's skills and intelligence may be advanced through effort, commitment, and tenacity. People who have a growth mindset are more inclined to welcome difficulties, learn from mistakes, and see feedback as a chance to get better.

People with a fixed mentality, in contrast, think that their skills and intellect are unchangeable, permanent qualities. They could fear taking chances, perceive problems as threats to their self-worth, and give up readily when faced with difficulties. As a result, adopting a growth mindset is crucial to laying a solid foundation for success.

Focusing on the present moment is a crucial component in developing a positive mentality and attitude. Many individuals frequently become mired in regrets from the past or fears about the future, which causes tension, worry, and unhappiness. Instead, staying grounded, reducing stress, and raising happiness may be achieved by concentrating on the present moment.

Being mindfully present in the moment may be developed through the practice of mindfulness meditation. When practicing mindfulness meditation, one focuses on the situation at hand without passing judgment or becoming distracted by ideas or feelings. People who regularly practice mindfulness meditation might become more optimistic and upbeat about life.

People may establish a good mentality and attitude by practicing appreciation in addition to having a development mindset and living in the present. Being appreciative of what one has rather than concentrating on what one lacks is a key component of gratitude. According to research, cultivating thankfulness may enhance relationships, happiness, and even physical health.

Keeping a gratitude diary and listing the things you are grateful for each day can be a simple way to practice gratitude. Spending time every day thinking about and expressing one's thanks to others is another technique to cultivate gratitude.

Finally, surrounding oneself with good influences is crucial for developing a positive mindset and attitude. This involves surrounding oneself with uplifting, motivating, and supportive others. Consuming uplifting media like books, podcasts, and other media that inspire and drive people toward their objectives is also a part of it.

In a nutshell, cultivating a good mindset and attitude is essential to laying a solid foundation for prosperity. This entails developing a development mentality, being present in the moment, being grateful, and surrounding oneself with inspiring people. People may overcome challenges, deal with adversity, and accomplish their goals and desires by cultivating these habits, which will result in a better, more fulfilled life.

Building a solid foundation is crucial for obtaining prosperity. This foundation goes beyond simply possessing the necessary abilities, information, or resources. It also involves cultivating a positive outlook and attitude that will enable you to overcome obstacles and accomplish your objectives.

How do mindsets work?

Our perceptions of ourselves and the world around us are shaped by our collective beliefs, thoughts, and attitudes, or mindset. It affects how we act and make decisions, which eventually affects how successful we are in life. In her book "Mindset: The New Psychology of Success," psychologist Carol Dweck popularized the idea of mindset. She distinguishes between fixed mindsets and development mindsets as the two main categories of mindsets.

A fixed mentality is the conviction that our intelligence, skills, and talents are unchangeable and permanent traits. People with fixed mindsets frequently shy away from difficulties and give up readily when they encounter them. They tend to take criticism personally and think that failure is a reflection on their qualities.

A growth mindset, on the other hand, is the conviction that we can improve our skills and abilities through effort, education, and persistence. Challenges are welcomed by those with a growth mentality, and they view failure as a chance to improve. In the face of obstacles and criticism, they are tenacious and resilient.

Why is a positive outlook crucial for prosperity?

Building a solid base for prosperity requires having a growth mentality. It enables you to overcome challenges, learn from mistakes, and acquire new knowledge and skills. You are more inclined to take chances, look for new possibilities, and pursue your objectives fervently and tenaciously if you have a growth mentality.

A stuck attitude, on the other hand, might prevent you from reaching your greatest potential. It could leave you feeling helpless and resigned to your situation. You could be less willing to experiment, try something new, or follow your aspirations.

How can I cultivate a development mindset?

The process of acquiring a development mindset takes time. Consistent effort and a willingness to question your ideas and presumptions are necessary. Here are some methods to help you cultivate a development mindset:

Accept challenges. Challenges should not be avoided but rather welcomed as chances to improve and learn. Seek opportunities to push yourself and accept new challenges that will enable you to gain new knowledge and skills.

Understand failure. Consider failure as a chance to learn and get better rather than as a personal reflection on your skills. Consider what went wrong, what to change going forward, and how you may learn from the event.

Develop a passion for learning. Create a zest for learning and actively seek out new information and abilities. Attend seminars, read books, take courses, and hang around with individuals that push you to grow.

Strive to be persistent. Faced with obstacles and challenges, cultivate resiliency and tenacity. Even when it's challenging or sluggish to make progress, keep at it.

What does "attitude" mean?

Another crucial element for laying a solid foundation for prosperity is attitude. It describes how we go about living, as well as how we see the world and how we react to it. Our attitude, which may be either positive or negative, greatly affects our conduct, interpersonal connections, and general success in life.

<u>Why is a positive mindset crucial for prosperity?</u>

Gaining prosperity requires having an optimistic outlook. In the face of obstacles and setbacks, it supports your ability to remain inspired, upbeat, and resilient. Additionally, it facilitates the development of solid connections, effective communication, and a network of like-minded individuals who support your objectives and ideals.

Creating a Personal Vision and Mission Statement for Prosperity

A potent practice that may direct people toward prosperity is developing a personal vision and mission statement. One may have a clear direction for their life and make practical efforts to build a successful future by clearly articulating their purpose, values, and ambitions.

A personal vision statement outlines the future that the individual wants to build for themselves. It is a long-term objective or dream that provides one with guidance and motivation. Imagine your goals, the sort of person you want to become, and the way you want to live your life as you write your personal vision statement. It must be interesting, exciting, and motivating enough to spur action toward realizing it.

One must begin by asking themselves some fundamental questions about their life before developing a personal vision statement for success, such as:

What goals do I have for my life?

What sort of individual do I hope to be?

What type of life am I looking for?

What are my fundamental beliefs and values?

What inspires and drives me?

One might begin creating their own vision statement based on the responses to these questions.

An illustration of a personal vision statement for prosperity is:

> *"I want to live a life of richness and satisfaction, where I'm spiritually connected, emotionally satisfied, and financially secure. I want to be a prosperous entrepreneur who develops ground-breaking solutions to pressing issues and has a beneficial influence on the world. I desire to have a meaningful life filled with opportunities for growth and service to others."*

Making a mission statement comes after coming up with a personal vision statement. A mission statement outlines one's purpose, beliefs, and objectives. It is a brief, precise, and unambiguous declaration of one's goals, plans for achieving those goals, and principles that they will uphold along the way.

The first step in writing a mission statement for prosperity is to identify your purpose, values, and objectives. A mission statement for prosperity may read, for instance:

> *"It is my goal to help others live prosperous lives by leading a purposeful, honest, and passionate existence. By developing original solutions that tackle significant issues and have a positive effect on the world, I will achieve financial affluence. I'll*

*have a fulfilling life by advancing my knowledge,
expanding my horizons, and helping others. In all
of my interactions, I will respect the principles of
truthfulness, sincerity, and kindness while working
to improve the world for both myself and others."*

A personal mission statement is a call to action as well as a declaration. It ought to spur action toward pursuing one's objectives and upholding one's values. To make choices and conduct activities that are consistent with one's purpose, beliefs, and goals, one should constantly examine their personal mission statement.

In conclusion, creating a personal vision and purpose statement is a powerful activity that may direct people toward success. Although it necessitates in-depth reflection and self-awareness, the advantages are enormous. One may have a clear direction for their life and make practical efforts to build a successful future by clearly articulating their purpose, values, and ambitions. A person's personal purpose and vision statement for success should be captivating, inspirational, and able to spur them on to action. A person's purpose, beliefs, and goals should also be frequently examined and utilized as a guide while making decisions and taking actions.

Summary

L iving a full and abundant life is the most fundamental human desire. However, finding one's way to wealth is not always simple. Through planning and effort, anyone may achieve unimaginable achievements with the help of this book. Part one of the power of planning is the first step in developing a plan for success is defining it for yourself. The final step is to break down your goals into manageable tasks.

The focusing power is part two. Eliminating interruptions is crucial for success. Eliminating distractions is the first step in developing concentration. The most crucial information in this work is how to get rid of distractions and other obstacles that stand in the way of achievement, such as fear and a lack of resources. The strategies for removing roadblocks to achievement, such as fear, a lack of financing, hurdles, and failures, are the most crucial information in this book. One of the most common hurdles is fear, so it's critical to face it head-on and take action to overcome it. Another frequent obstacle is a lack of cash; therefore, it's critical to have inventive solutions on hand to overcome it.

Failures and obstacles are commonplace on the road to success, so it's critical to learn from them and use what you can to advance your development. The need for lifelong learning is also discussed, and being informed is one of the best ways to stay current. A state of enjoyment, success, and riches, prosperity encompasses a wide variety of aspects of life, including material prosperity, personal growth, and societal advancement. Given that having access to resources and financial stability are crucial components of a happy life, they are related to an expanding economy and financial prosperity. It also includes personal growth and fulfillment, as well as societal development and the welfare of others.

Financial stability is not the only aspect of life covered by the multifaceted concept of prosperity. Prosperity is a subjective term that varies from person to person. People and communities need to invest in education and skill development, support entrepreneurship and innovation, and create a more inclusive and just society if they want to succeed.

They must also encourage sustainable development, which eliminates poverty and inequality while safeguarding the environment for future generations. People must identify the facets of life that are most important to them and take action to make them a reality in order to construct their own definition of success.

Setting their own standards for success provides them with direction and concentration, empowering them to set goals and move toward them with purpose. You can stay motivated and conquer obstacles by clearly knowing what success means to you individually. You can live a meaningful life and act in a way that is consistent with your values when you are aware of what is important to you. Success and happiness depend on having a clear understanding of wealth because it provides focus, motivation, direction, and a sense of purpose.

The most crucial information in this text is the value of having clear financial goals, the role of positive thinking and visualization in success, the effectiveness of routines and habits in success, the value of self-discipline in success, the value of perseverance and determination in success, and the value of a growth mindset in success. Perseverance and determination are two traits that are necessary for success. While resolve is the capacity to put up the necessary effort and labor, despite probable hurdles, to achieve one's goals, perseverance is the capacity to maintain momentum and advancement toward one's goals. Success in every pursuit, whether it be in business, athletics, education, or interpersonal relationships, requires perseverance and drive. Success in all areas of life—whether it is business, athletics, education, or interpersonal relationships—requires tenacity and perseverance. Through networking, you may meet new people, learn about market trends, and become knowledgeable about your industry. Every effective cooperation is built on relationships and being able to establish credibility and gain the trust of people through making solid connections may lead to new opportunities and collaborations. By establishing contacts and networking, you may increase your chances of success in a number of areas, including job search and business growth.

Achieving success in both one's personal and professional lives requires networking. It may increase a company's market reach and speed up its development, provide you access to seasoned professionals for mentoring and assistance, increase your visibility and make you more recognizable in your industry, and help you build a strong personal brand. You may increase your success, find new opportunities, and create long-lasting partnerships that can aid your business or profession through networking and building relationships. Success in both one's personal and professional lives depends on ongoing learning and self-improvement. One of the key benefits of continual learning and self-improvement is being able to keep up with the most recent advancements and trends in one's career.

The benefits of lifelong learning and growth for achieving achievement are the most significant information in this work. Lifelong learning may boost productivity and effectiveness in daily life, broaden perspectives, and give individuals a greater awareness of the world around them. It can also help people adjust to changing circumstances and grab new opportunities as they arise. Additionally, it may have a significant impact on a person's growth by broadening their perspectives and raising their standard of living generally. Despite these challenges, lifelong learning and self-improvement are benefits that make the effort worthwhile. It's vital to keep in mind that while lifelong learning and self-improvement might occasionally be challenging, the benefits outweigh the challenges.

Making a commitment to lifelong learning and improving oneself is crucial for overcoming anxiety and uncertainty when pursuing success. The techniques described in this book for overcoming anxieties and uncertainties related to realizing our full potential are the most crucial information. These include identifying our fears and uncertainties, establishing acceptable goals, developing a plan, acting, accepting failure, getting help, and taking care of oneself. The key to overcoming fear and uncertainty is to identify our worries and uncertainties, set realistic goals, develop a plan, act, accept failure, get help, and practice self-care. It's critical to act, accept failure, ask for help, and practice self-care if you want to succeed.

The most significant information in this book emphasizes how crucial it is to take reasonable risks in order to flourish. Taking calculated risks entails comparing the chances of success against the possibility of failure, calculating the benefits and drawbacks of the situation, and gathering relevant information. Successful entrepreneurs frequently take calculated risks to grow their businesses, such as investing in a new product line or taking on a challenging project. Success may also come from taking measured risks with one's money, such as investing in the stock market or starting a business. The most significant information in this work is that taking calculated risks is necessary for leading a successful life and that doing so involves careful consideration, weighing the pros and cons, and deliberate decision-making. It might lead to success and prosperity in a number of areas of life, such as work, relationships, wealth, and personal growth. People need to learn to identify their beliefs and spend some time reflecting on their attitudes, behaviors, and cognitive processes in order to identify and get rid of limiting concepts that inhibit financial success. This will assist them in identifying and eradicating limiting beliefs that obstruct their ability to succeed financially.

The actions that can be taken to improve one's quality of life are the most significant information in this book. These actions include challenging restrictive ideas, switching them out for freeing ones, taking action, and surrounding oneself with inspiring people.

When challenging limiting beliefs, one must ask whether they are true and whether there is any evidence to support them. Adopt the notion that money flows to you swiftly and in abundance to replace restrictive thoughts with freeing ones. Set goals that are in line with your new beliefs and take action to achieve them to move forward.

Spend time with inspiring individuals to reinforce your new beliefs and keep yourself motivated to reach your goals.

Lastly, attend seminars, listen to podcasts, or read books that promote growth-oriented thinking. For people, businesses, and communities as a whole to succeed, innovation and creativity are two crucial components. While creativity is the ability to come up with original ideas, solutions, and approaches to problems, innovation is the process of translating ideas into practical applications that benefit society. When innovation and creativity are encouraged, it may lead to better living circumstances, expanding economies, and increased levels of productivity.

By generating novel products and services that benefit society, innovation and creativity increase productivity, open up new markets and job opportunities, and enhance social and environmental conditions. In a highly competitive market, businesses must create distinctive products to stay one step ahead of their competitors. A more diverse and dynamic workforce will arise from innovation and creativity, which may also attract both domestic and foreign investment. Innovation and creativity may lead to the establishment of new markets and job opportunities. The most crucial information in this book is that innovation and creativity must be supported by governments, corporations, and the general public in order for success to be possible in today's world of rapid change. It's crucial to believe in oneself, set clear goals, nurture optimism, and see failure as a necessary step on the path to success in order to develop a success mentality for monetary gain.

Confidence in oneself, setting clear goals, cultivating an upbeat mindset, and accepting failure as a necessary step on the path to success are all crucial for success. The guidelines for developing a successful mindset are the most crucial information in this book. These values involve embracing failure and viewing it as a chance to succeed, developing a growth mindset, hanging out with inspiring people, and acting to accomplish goals. Additionally, appreciation and thankfulness may have a big impact on a lot of things in life, including how successful we can be. Enjoying plenty in all areas of life, such as health, relationships, and personal growth, is what prosperity is all about.

We may shift our focus from what we lack to what we currently have and make room for even more abundance to enter our lives by practicing gratitude and appreciation. Finally, by focusing on our blessings, we train our thoughts to see the positive side of any situation. Having a grateful attitude is crucial for attracting more positive opportunities and experiences into our lives. It can also assist us in getting past challenges and roadblocks. By expressing our gratitude, we are reminded of all the blessings in our lives and given the willpower and strength to carry on.

Gratitude may also improve our view of life and the quality of our relationships with others. By expressing our gratitude and appreciation to others, we fortify our relationships and create an atmosphere of respect and trust. By praising others' achievements, we begin a constructive cycle of reciprocity in which everyone gains from the group's success. Finally, gratitude can enable us to maximize the resources and possibilities at our disposal in order to double our wealth. Increasing prosperity requires appreciation and gratitude.

Gratitude supports us in adopting a positive mindset, overcoming challenges, improving our relationships, and living more fulfilling lives. Appreciation enables us to create a positive energy momentum that propels us toward our goals and desires. We may have more meaningful and contented lives by practicing appreciation and gratitude. We get a sense of fulfillment and purpose that surpasses material wealth by leading an appreciative life.

Please use this book as your guide on your path to prosperity.

What Next?

Ready to put this knowledge to work?

Check out Unlock Wealth— a guided journal designed to help you break free from money stress, gain clarity on your financial goals, track your progress, and finally take control of your money so you can build a life you love.

Unlock Wealth – Out Now.
Unlock Fortune — Coming Spring 2026!

About the Author

TJ Hill

TJ Hill never imagined she'd become an author. Her journey started in business consulting, where she spent years helping entrepreneurs and their teams build stronger, smoother operations. Along the way, she noticed something surprising: no matter how successful people looked on the outside, many of them felt overwhelmed when it came to managing their money.

That realization changed everything. TJ saw that what people needed wasn't complicated financial talk—they needed simple, step-by-step guidance that actually fit into real life. So she set out to create books, journals, and guides that would make money management less intimidating and far more empowering.

Her mission is simple: to help readers feel confident with their finances, take control of their money, and build the future they deserve. Through her writing, TJ shares encouragement, clarity, and a reminder that financial freedom isn't just for a few—it's possible for anyone willing to take the first step.

You can find all of her books and journals at https://tjhillbooks.com/